Help Me Remember

BIBLE STORIES FOR CHILDREN

Elaine Blanchard

THE
PILGRIM
PRESS
Cleveland

This work is dedicated to my partner, Anna Neal.
I have found a home in her love and faithfulness.

The Pilgrim Press, 700 Prospect Avenue, Cleveland, Ohio 44115-1100, thepilgrimpress.com
© 2005 by Elaine Blanchard

All rights reserved. Published 2005

Biblical quotations are from the New Revised Standard Version of the Bible © copyright 1989 by
the Division of Christian Education of the National Council of the Churches of Christ in the U.S.A., and are
used by permission.

Printed in the United States of America on acid-free paper

10   09   08   07   06   05   5   4   3   2   1

Library of Congress Cataloging-in-Publication Data

Blanchard, Elaine, 1952-
    Help me Remember : Bible stories for children / Elaine Blanchard.
        p.   cm.
    ISBN 0-8298-1600-3 (pbk. : alk. paper)
    1. Bible stories, English.   I. Title.

BS550.3.B545   2005
220.9'505—dc22

                                                                        2004063774

Contents

Preface

The Christian family is a family built on stories. Our identity has been shaped by stories told and retold. Before we had the printed text that we now know as the Old and New Testaments, we had stories. They were told at tables, around fires, and from nomadic tribes into the agricultural communities. Generation after generation heard the stories told before the stories were captured and held by print. Our stories shape a particular understanding of our heritage, family expectations, and possibilities for the future of our family.

When we fail to tell the stories to our children, we lose a piece of our heritage as a storytelling family. When we refuse to allow the stories to be fluid, to have a creative flow between the story and the storyteller, we rob the stories of their life and power.

We remain free to be a people of stories, to trust that God's creative forces are at work as today's storytellers pass along our stories. The Christian family is a creative family, blessed with imagination. Our vision of the new heaven and the new earth is created by the gift of human imagination and empowered by God's Holy Spirit.

I have taken creative liberty with many of the stories held in this printed collection. I learned the stories of our faith in Sunday school. I now tell the stories to children who have very different experiences than I did when I first heard these stories. The children of today have a different understanding of their own heritage, family expectations, and possibilities for the future than I did in the 1950s when I read my Sunday school papers and colored the outlined pictures inside them. This is the age of information. Our children know more than we could possibly have known at the same age.

It is my hope that by sharing these stories I will give creative energy to those who tell the stories and to those who hear them. I have not set out to share information but to share from my soul. I suspect the original Hebrew storytellers allowed their stories to speak to the moment and the people who heard the stories. The human imagination set free to dream and create can inspire great hope for us and for our families.

I pass along these stories with an invitation to those who read them. Share the stories as you are moved to share them. Let them come alive in you and you will receive new life. I look into the eyes of the children who listen to the stories and I learn from them. Those who sit in front of you will feel your enthusiasm for the creative process at work and they will receive hope along with the story. In the words of John Robinson, an important character in the shaping of Congregationalism, "The Lord hath yet more light and truth to break forth from his holy word."

Acknowledgements

I share these stories with deep gratitude to the terrific people at First Congregational Church in Memphis, Tennessee. I am particularly grateful to Rev. Cheryl Cornish, our pastor. Her preaching and leadership skills have created a miraculous environment. The people of First Congregational UCC Church are my family. I feel proud to belong to a congregation so alive, courageous, committed, and creative. They have heard my stories and asked for more. I have been inspired by their encouragement and love.

My friends, Michael and Steve, deserve thanks. Steve Klinkerman went with me to purchase my first computer and then taught me how to use it. Michael Schiefelbein, as a writer, a teacher, and a beautiful friend, is truly an inspiration for my creative work.

1

It Is All Good

GENESIS 1:1–31

Once, a very long time ago, even before your own mother and father were born, there was only God. No one knows how long this had been going on since there was only God and no one kept time.

Then, no one but God knows why, God felt tired of being the only thing that was. God decided to get a job and decided to get very busy making new things. It was magnificent work!

First God made the light of day and the dark of night. That was a good thing since that made it possible for us to know when to get up and when to go to bed. It also made it possible for us to count the days so that we would know when to celebrate our birthday each year.

Then God busily made the waters: puddles, ponds, lakes, rivers, and the great swelling seas. Then God made dry land: rolling plains, deserts, hills, and the tall mountains. God worked over the surface of the earth until the water and the dry land were separate things. God spread the sky above it all like a lovely scarf on a woman's head. It was good to look up into the rich blue of the sky. It was good to look at the cool water and the warm, dry land. God enjoyed being at work. God clapped with delight and winds formed. They wrapped themselves around the earth like belts.

Then God made plants of every kind: grass, flowers, spinach, oats, and pine trees. God put seeds into the wet and dry land so that plants could grow everywhere. Plants and trees swayed in the wind, dancing and entertaining God as God continued to work.

God made animals. Birds with wings flew into the air. Four-legged creatures with warm and beautiful fur ran across the land. Fish slapped their tails and swam quickly through the waters. God was so excited about the good work that God reached out and hugged the neck of a nice, soft giraffe. Some things, like joy, are just meant to be shared!

Then God took a deep breath and breathed it into the next creation: boys and girls. This was an excellent thing for God to do. God created boys and girls with brains so that they could think about the sky, the earth, the water, the birds, the furry animals, and the fish. Boys and girls could think and decide how they wanted to treat the other things God had made. God put love into the minds and bodies of boys and girls so that they could choose to share the best of themselves with creation, with one another, and with God. They were each given the gift of gratitude so that they could say, "Thanks!" to God for the beauty of all things and for life itself.

Finally the work was complete and God was tired. It was time for a day off. With uplifted hands, God shaped a big red rubber ball, which was carried into a lovely field. The field was covered with warm breezes and colorful wild flowers. God invited all the boys and girls to gather in the field for a game of ball. They all played together in the sun. Everyone laughed, sweated, ran, and fell down many times. God roared with the good time they had together. It was great fun.

God took time, after the game, to sit under a tree. God looked around, and gave a happy grin. "It is good," God whispered to the gathered children. A soft brown rabbit snuggled down into God's lap and went to sleep. God gently petted the rabbit's ears and back. "It is good." Everyone in the field agreed with God. God gave each person a red, shiny apple to eat. In between munches, they all said, "It is good. It is all good isn't it?"

Will you help me remember, especially when someone you know is having a hard time feeling good about him- or herself and the world around us, that God made the whole world and said that it is good? It is all good.

2

Floating on the Flood

GENESIS 7:1–24, 8:1–22

A very long, long time ago there was a man named Mr. Noah who pleased God. Now this was at a time when not much on the earth was pleasing God. In fact, God was wondering if creating the world had been such a good idea afterall. People were not behaving well. They were violent, damaging themselves and others. People had forgotten that they were created to love and care for the earth, themselves and each other.

So God spoke to the man who pleased him and said, "Mr. Noah, I intend to have a cleaning day. I need your help with this plan. Please build a huge ark and get ready for rain." Mr. Noah thought this was a strange request from God since there was not a cloud in the sky. But Mr. Noah was a very good man who always did what God asked him to do, so he went to the Home Depot and got hammers and nails, quite a lot of cypress wood and pitch (which is like tar), to keep the water from coming inside the ark. On the way home, he stopped at the grocery and got a few things for Mrs. Noah. He also bought a few large umbrellas.

Well, God and Mr. Noah worked closely together, God giving the design and Mr. Noah putting the ark together. As Mr. Noah sawed and hammered, God explained the situation. "I am going to flood everything on the earth. You and your family will float on top of the water. You will be busy while it rains. You and your family will have many animals to feed and many messes to clean up on the floor of the ark. I want you to bring along pairs, male and female, of each animal and bird. Of the animals you eat, you will bring along seven pairs.

You have seven days to get them on the ark with you and then the rain will begin. It will rain for forty days and forty nights. This flood will destroy every living thing on earth. But I will make a promise to you and to your family. We will be partners in the cleaned-up creation." Mr. Noah kept working while God spoke, trying to ignore the neighbors and townspeople who were standing around laughing and hooting, making fun of Mr. Noah for building a boat and getting ready for a flood when there was not a drop of rain in sight.

Mr. Noah and his family gathered all the animals (eagles, sparrows, mice, tigers, elephants, and turtles) just like God had said to do. Mrs. Noah fussed around, providing fresh towels and making sure all the animals had a nice place to stay on the ark. The three sons of Mr. and Mrs. Noah came on board along with their wives. They all had work to do. There were many plants to bring on board. Many baskets filled with food. Hay bale after hay bale was lugged up the ramp. Let me tell you that nobody in the Noah family had any trouble sleeping that night!

Then "the fountains of the great deep burst forth, and the windows of the heavens were opened." That's what it says in the Bible. The rains fell for forty days and the ark was lifted higher and higher on top of the flood. If anybody in the neighborhood was laughing at Mr. Noah, the laughter could not be heard for the rain, the rushing water, and the winds. After the rains stopped, the waters continued to swell on the face of the earth for another one hundred and ten days. And that's quite a long time for any living thing to live under water. I think it is impossible for anything other than fish.

Mr. Noah and his family had plenty to do on that ark...pitching hay, cleaning out stalls, frying fish for themselves, running laps to stay in shape. There were many evenings when all the work was done and the sons of Mr. Noah rode the ponies while Mr. and Mrs. Noah played checkers by candlelight. Months went by, even after the ark settled on top of a mountain. Still, the waters were overwhelming and everyone stayed on board with the birds, animals, and potted plants.

One day Mr. Noah opened a window and let in a breath of fresh air. He sent a raven out to fly back and forth. Back and forth. Then he sent a dove. The dove came back to the ark because it was the only place the bird could find to land. Days later, Mr. Noah sent another dove out to have a look around and that dove returned with an olive leaf in its beak. This told Mr.

Noah that dry ground was not far away.

A few weeks later, Mr. Noah lifted the cover off the top of the ark and saw dry ground. God was right there, directing Mr. Noah and his family to step out and to bring the animals with them. So "every animal, every creeping thing, and every bird, everything that moves on the earth, went out of the ark by families." Mr. Noah built an altar and knelt down, giving thanks to God for life and for the privilege of being in partnership with God.

That's when God placed the rainbow in the sky, a gorgeous display of colors stretched from one end of the earth to the other. It amazed the Noah family to see it. God explained that this beautiful sight was a sign of God's promise to live and work in partnership and in love with Noah and his family forever and ever and ever and ever. God said, "When I see this rainbow, I will remember my covenant with you and all of your descendants. The waters shall never again become a flood to destroy all the earth."

I am going to remember Mr. Noah the next time I see a rainbow. I'm going to remember the power and the promise of God's partnership with creation and with us. We are descendants of Mr. and Mrs. Noah ourselves, you know? Will you help me remember?

3

Abram and Sarai

GENESIS 12:1–9

A very long time ago, long after Noah's ark settled down on dry ground, the earth was rich with plants and animals. The flood was only a memory, a story that grandparents told the little children. Trees were tall and healthy again. Birds sang from the limbs of olive branches and built nests for their babies. Noah's three sons were growing older in the shade of those olive trees. Their names were Shem, Ham, and Japheth. The sons of Noah had many children and their children had many children. They all lived together and enjoyed raising babies, working in the fields, and growing older. The sun warmed them and warmed their animals. It warmed the grain right up out of the ground. They ate well together and enjoyed prosperity. They looked to God and gave thanks for all that they had. God was glad to be close friends with this family.

One day God looked at the family of Abram, one of Noah's grandsons, who was living with his wife in a land called Haran.

God spoke to Abram while Abram was sitting outside his tent enjoying an afternoon breeze. God said, "Leave the land of Haran. Take your wife Sarai, and your animals. Start walking and follow me."

Abram stood up and looked out into the desert in front of him. The sand hills were high and he could see only so far into the distance. He had no idea what might be beyond the farthest point his eyes could see. "Where am I going?" Abram asked God. "I am already seventy-five years old. I'm already weak with old age."

"You are going where I will lead you, to a land called Canaan." God answered. Abram thought for a while. His wife, Sarai, might not be happy if she had to start walking away from her home and out to a place Abram could not describe for her. He knew that God had always been very good to him and to Sarai. But this was a difficult request. Abram was scared. "I'll follow you, God," he spoke carefully. "But help me explain this to Sarai." Abram was a man who loved his wife and loved to see her happy.

When Sarai heard that they were moving, she asked a few questions. "What about our sheep and goats?" Sarai was a woman who loved the furry creatures in the yard and in the field. Abram told her that the animals were traveling with them.

"Who will help you set up our tent when night comes and we need a place to rest?" Abram told her that he planned to take his nephew, Lot, with them as they followed God.

Sarai began to pack her cooking things, her pots and pans.

Abram began taking down the tent they called home. Lot came over that afternoon. He had said, "Good-bye," to his mother and father. They were worried about Lot but they let him go because, whether they wanted to let Lot go away or not, they trusted God.

The three travelers started out, leaving home and family behind. God spoke to Abram as the old man put one tired foot in front of the other. "God said, "I will bless you, Abram, in the land of Canaan. I will make your family large there. People will know your name and you will be a blessing to your new neighbors and friends." Abram heard what God said.

He was trying to be brave. But he did not know what his new home would be like. He hoped Sarai and Lot would be safe and happy there. He kept walking, moving toward Canaan, only because God had called him to go there.

When they arrived in Canaan, Abram was delighted! His fear began to disappear. The sun was warm there. The palm trees were swaying in the breeze over ponds of cool water where his animals took a drink. Olive trees were full to overflowing with big, juicy olives. Sarai looked happy and Lot sat down to rest. Abram looked up and thanked God for the beauty of this land. He built a monument there to honor God's friendship with Abram.

You know you could build your own monument! Gather some stones. Share the stone gathering with some of your friends. Then, in a safe and sacred place, stack the stones into a monument; let that place be where you remember to honor your friendship with

God. The monument Abram created, marked the place God called him to be. Abram worshiped God wherever God led him. Every Sunday we worship the God of Abram and renew our promise to live in faith with God. Each of you follows God to church. You bring your trust in God with you and that is a gift to God and a gift to all of us who worship with you.

God was grateful for Abram's faith. It was a gift from this old man. And God said, "Thank you." Abram was surprised to hear God thanking him. But God kept on talking, "You will be remembered forever as the man who trusted God. Other people will find the courage they need to have faith and trust because of your story. I am going to give you and your wife new names along with your new home. You will be known as Abraham instead of Abram. Sarai's name will now be Sarah."

I am going to try to remember the faith of Abraham and Sarah and Lot. Sometimes God calls us to do new things or to go to new places. I feel scared sometimes. We learn to like what we know as home, the friends we have, and the places we go. But will you help me to remember that I can trust God like Abram and Sarai trusted God? I can simply follow where God leads, putting one foot in front of the other. God is always the same, familiar and kind. God goes with us into the new places and situations. It helps us to have other people trusting God as we travel together. I'll try to help you to remember to trust if you'll help me to remember too.

4

Sodom and Gomorrah

GENESIS 18:16–19:29

On a long, hot afternoon, many years ago, when Abraham was sitting outside his tent and enjoying some refreshments with guests who had dropped by for the day, God spoke to Abraham. The guests were waving good-bye and heading toward a city known as Sodom when Abraham heard God talking about punishment. God was not pleased with the people of Sodom and so God planned to get their attention by destroying the city. Abraham winced at the thought. Abraham's nephew, Lot, lived close to the gates of Sodom. Abraham didn't want Lot or Lot's family to be destroyed. He felt scared of God's anger. "Couldn't you spare the city, God? What if there are fifty really good people in the city? What about them? Would you destroy them with those who have behaved badly?"

God thought about what Abraham had said. God was a God of justice. God replied, "If I find fifty righteous people, I will forgive the entire city for the sake of those who are righteous."

Then Abraham began bargaining with God, pleading for the people of Sodom. "What if there are only forty righteous people?" God thought some more and decided to spare the city for forty righteous people.

Abraham scratched his beard and asked, "Well, what if there were thirty righteous people, would you forgive the whole city of Sodom for their sake?" God agreed to it. Abraham felt sorry for the people who were his neighbors. He didn't really know them but he cared about them all the same. "What if there are twenty righteous people? Would that number of good people be enough to cause you, God, to forgive the entire city?" God agreed to it.

Abraham took his hat and held it in his hand as he looked to God with fear and hope in his eyes. "God, what if only ten righteous people can be found in the whole city of Sodom? Would you forgive the people and have mercy on Sodom for the sake of those ten good people?" God agreed. God turned and walked away from Abraham. God was tired of thinking about it, and Abraham went back to his tent where he took an afternoon nap.

Meanwhile, at the city gates of Sodom, guests were arriving. Two men, dusty and tired from traveling a great distance, were about to knock on the gate when they noticed Lot sitting in the shade of an olive tree with his sheep wandering around. (You remember Lot, don't you? He is the nephew of Abraham, the one who left Haran with his Aunt Sarai and Uncle Abram.) Lot invited the two strangers to his home for dinner. "Let me wash your feet and give you a bed to sleep on tonight." Lot was always happy to have company. Guests could tell exciting stories of other places and other people. Lot stood up and led the guests to his home. He broke off some bread for the two men and they dipped it in olive oil. Lot poured some herbal tea for his guests. They were enjoying themselves, just beginning to tell Lot a good story, when they heard a noise outside.

The old men and the young men from the city of Sodom were standing in a crowd outside Lot's door. It was an awful sight! The men of Sodom were wearing torn and stained robes. Their beards were long and matted with bits of greasy food caught in the tangles. Their teeth were yellow and decayed. They carried long sharp sticks, spears, and knives with them. They growled in a chorus outside the door. GRRRRRRRRRR!

Lot put his bread and tea cup on the table and noticed that his knees were rat-a-tat-tatting under his robe. He wanted to hide in the closet but he knew he had to protect his guests. It was the honorable thing to do. He took a deep breath and opened the door and walked out smiling with a rather wobbly smile. "What is the matter?" he asked the growling crowd.

"We do not like strangers coming around with their different way of talking and their different way of thinking. We saw you inviting strangers into your home. Now let us in or bring those men out here. We plan to kill them before they try to change us in any way. GRRRRRRR!" Flies swarmed from their heads as they shook their sticks, knives, and spears in Lot's face.

Now Lot knew that the men of Sodom, both old and young, were not very well mannered people. They drank too much ale and they didn't even try to learn very much at school. Lot knew the Sodomites were a rough bunch but he was shocked to hear them threaten to kill two innocent guests in his home. "Look," he was thinking quickly, "I have two daughters who have had dancing lessons. One of my servants can play the harp while my wife and I keep time with tambourines. It will be fun. You will be well entertained! Then you fellows can go back home and sleep this day away. You'll feel better tomorrow."

But the men from Sodom were not listening. They had their chins aimed toward the opening in Lot's front door. They rushed toward the door just as the strangers inside (who were, by the way, angels sent by God) reached out with expand-o arms and quickly snatched Lot by the neck. They dragged him inside to safety. Then they slammed the door shut. Fast!

The men of Sodom were trying to break the door down when the two guests zapped all of them blind. They could not see! So the nasty crowd of men stumbled blindly, bumping into each other, falling down and rolling around, toward the city gates, wondering what in the world had just happened.

Lot and his guests resumed their tea drinking and bread breaking. The men asked Lot and his wife, "Do you have any family in or near this city of Sodom or in the next city, called Gomorrah? If you do, we need to get them out of the way because God is planning to destroy both of these cities. The men of the cities are mean. They treat strangers badly. You have seen it with your own eyes and witnessed the ugliness. Now be prepared to run away, up into the hills, where you and all of your family will be safe."

Lot, who was tired of traveling and moving to new places, was hesitant. "I don't like living in the hills. It's hot and lonely there. The land does not provide enough grass for my sheep and goats. Can't I go over to the little city beyond the hills? It's a place where people remember how to be kind to strangers."

"Yes. Yes! You can go to the little city beyond the hills. Only gather your family and go quickly before the destruction begins. You do not want to be near Sodom and Gomorrah.

"The men there have never learned to trust God. They do not share their gifts with God or with anyone. Because they have no trust, they have grown twisted and mean, frightened of anything different than themselves."

Lot got his daughters, their husbands, his wife and his herds of sheep and goats altogether. The group ran as fast as they could run up to the hills and then over them. As they got to the top of the hill, Lot's wife looked back over her shoulder. She remembered her friends in the city of Sodom, women and children she had known there. The backward gaze was painful for her. She saw quite clearly that good people, innocent women and children, can be hurt by the bad behavior of people around them. As she followed her husband into the little city over the hill, she thought about that. It was a painful thought for Lot's wife and that pain made her quite sad for the rest of her life. Her new friends in the city where she settled with Lot and her daughters said of her, "She turned into salt with that backward glance." They meant that she was never the same person as she had once been.

Will you help the people of your church to remember to trust in God and to treat strangers with kindness? Will you help your church to keep being a place of hospitality so that church people will always welcome strangers, even when the strangers come from far away places or have very different ways of talking and thinking than we do? We might be welcoming angels when we share our hospitality with strangers.

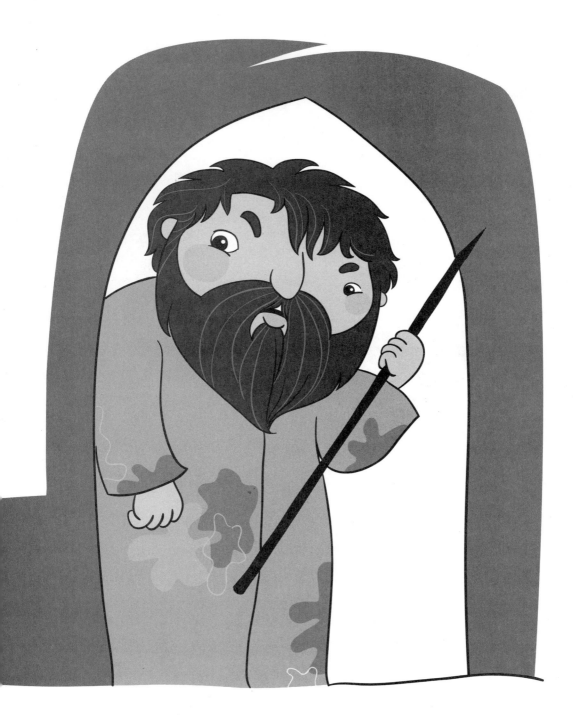

5

A Wife for Isaac

GENESIS 24

Abraham grew to be very old. He was a man who looked back over the years and felt grateful. He had many things about which to feel gratitude. He looked over his shoulder and saw Sarah mixing bread dough in a huge bowl. He loved her. He had loved her for many years. His wife had helped him through the bad times and had made the good times even better. He wanted his son, Isaac, to be able to look back over the years, when he grew to be an old man, and to be grateful as well. He hoped that Isaac would be in love with a wife of his own for a long, long time. Abraham talked to God about Isaac, asking God to provide a partner for his son, a wife who would love Isaac as Sarah had loved Abraham.

Then Abraham called his most trusted servant, Dan, to him and gave the servant instructions. It turned out that God had a plan for Isaac and God had shared that plan with Abraham. Isn't that amazing? Abraham heard God say that the wife for Isaac was living back in the land of Haran where Abraham and Sarah had lived before Isaac was born. So Abraham packed a huge bag of food for Dan and gave it to him, saying, "Go back to Haran and find the woman God has blessed to be the wife of my son, Isaac." That's just the way things were done back then. Odd to us but not so odd to the ancient people. Isaac would never have a date with his wife-to-be. They would never go to a movie together or attend a dance together before they were engaged. They would meet each other and marry each other. It was all arranged by God and their parents.

So the servant gathered gifts, things to impress even a princess, and he put the gifts on the camel's back. There were beads, bracelets, bangles, and baubles. There were jewels, perfumes, and dresses made of finest silk. Abraham's servant packed cookies and candy to make anyone's mouth water. Finally the camel could carry no more and so the servant set out. Abraham waved good-bye.

Dan rode along on his camel, kerplunk, kerplunk, over the dry and dusty desert toward the land of Haran. The sun was hot on his back and he was wilting just a little when a band of robbers came over a rise and tried to rob Dan of all the golden gifts he carried. Dan was given special powers from God. He zipped and zapped the staff he carried. Balls of fire exploded in the sky over head. That sent those robbers whimpering back over the hill as Dan and his camel kerplunk, kerplunked along.

Dan was singing a very nice song for his camel and rather

enjoying himself when a great windstorm blew into his face. It picked up the man and his camel and threw them up into the air. They might have been killed but an angel of God reached out and grabbed them from the windstorm's frenzy. Dan and his camel were safely placed back on the ground. The servant had to rest a while after that. He had to comb his hair back into place and straighten the camel's mane. But pretty soon he and his camel were kerplunking along, looking forward to meeting the woman God had chosen to be Isaac's wife.

As the sun was setting and the servant of Abraham was getting sleepy, he saw a city in the distance. He stopped his camel by the well outside the city and noticed that many women were walking to the well with water jugs. They were getting water for their families and leading animals to the well. That was once the daily chore for women. They made sure that everyone had enough water for the day. Sheep, goats, and camels were following the women to the water. Dan climbed down from his camel's back and watched from a distance.

The servant wanted to be sure that the woman he took back to be Isaac's wife was the woman God intended for Isaac to have as a wife. So he talked to God. "Show me the right woman, God. Here are many women and maybe one of them would be a good wife for my master's son. Isaac needs a wife who loves animals and is kind like his mother, Sarah. I will look for a woman like that and trust you to point her out to me."

Just then a beautiful young woman noticed Dan as she filled

her water jar. She had shiny black hair and beautiful brown eyes. She walked up to Dan and his camel and said, "I see you are a stranger here. Let me give you a drink of water." She offered him her drinking gourd.

Dan took a drink and talked silently to God. "That was nice. She seems like a kind woman. But how do I know that she is as nice and kind as Sarah?"

Just then the lovely young woman exclaimed, "Look! The poor animal has a rock in his pad!" She bent over and looked more closely at Dan's camel. Then she carefully removed a small stone from the pad on his foot. Dan watched as she washed the sore place and rubbed the camel's foot. The camel smiled broadly. All of this attention was making the camel feel proud! And Dan was smiling too because it seemed clear enough that this lovely young woman was as kind as Sarah ever was. "Let me give your camel a drink," she said. "Please lift this heavy pack from your camel's back. The two of you must rest. You can spend the night with my family. We have a nice stable for this poor tired creature."

"What is your name?" Dan asked her.

"I am Rebekah," she answered.

Dan took a gold nose-ring from the heavy pack. He took a gold and jeweled bracelet also. And he gave these gifts to Rebecca, saying, "Take these gifts home and tell your father I have come from the land of Canaan. I was sent by my master, Abraham, to find a wife for his son, Isaac."

Rebekah took the gifts and she went home quickly. ""Look!"

she called out to her family as she got close to her home, "Look at what a man at the well gave to me!"

Rebekah's father and brother went out to meet the stranger. They invited him to come home with them for the night. Everyone ate and rested well.

The next morning the servant of Abraham got out of bed and stretched his arms and legs in the warmth of the rising sun. As the family got up and began the day there was much talk among Dan, Rebekah's father, and her brother. The men made decisions in the family. Rebekah went on to the well and got water for her family while it was decided that she would ride, kerplunk, kerplunk, back across the desert with Dan. She would leave home and go to a new place where she would become the wife of Isaac and join his family in the land of Canaan. No one asked Rebekah if she liked the decision or if she wanted to be Isaac's wife. So it was a good thing that she was happy about going. She looked at all the fine gifts Dan had brought with him while her mother packed food for the long journey back to Canaan.

Then Rebekah put on one of her new silk dresses, dabbed perfume behind her ear and put the nose ring on. "Take me to my new husband!" she laughed. Her mother cried as Rebekah rode away on the back of Dan's camel.

So the two of them set out to return to the land where Abraham lived with his family. The journey was long and dusty. Rebekah and Dan were resting one evening, drinking cool water from a leather pouch, when a wolf came over the hill. It snarled and looked hungrily at the two tired travelers. Rebekah handed the drinking pouch to Dan and stepped toward the fierce looking creature. She put out her hand and spoke softly. Dan could not hear what she was saying but whatever she said must have been powerful in wolf language. The wolf stopped snarling and lay down in the sand with its snout between both front paws. Rebekah walked to the animal's side and petted it. Dan knew for certain he had the right woman to be Isaac's wife.

It was almost dark when they got close enough for Isaac to see them coming. He knew that Dan would be bringing a wife home. He had been waiting on a hill for many days. He combed his hair and straightened his robe. He popped a piece of mint into his mouth and stood up as tall as he could stand. He wanted to impress his wife-to-be.

Rebekah was looking too. She saw the young man standing on top of the hill. She asked the servant, "Who is that handsome man we see over there?"

The servant smiled a great big smile and answered her, "That handsome man will be your husband. He is Isaac."

Rebekah threw her head back and laughed with delight. Isaac began to run, hurrying to meet his beautiful, laughing wife-to-be. He helped her down from the camel's back and they looked closely at each other for the first time. They could see friendship and love in the eyes of the other. It was the beginning of a long and adventurous life together.

Finally came the wedding day. Abraham looked at his son's

happiness and the joy of his new daughter-in-law. He was grateful. God kept on giving good gifts to his family. Abraham enjoyed the blessings of God. He trusted God more and more as he became a very old man.

These people are special people in our family history. Abraham and Sarah, Isaac and Rebekah. They are people related to us by way of our faith. The trust that Abraham developed is a trust we can have too. It's a gift, a family heirloom, passed down from generation to generation. The children of Isaac and Rebekah learned to trust God and we learn to trust God too. Our trust is called faith. Will you help me to remember that?

6

Jacob and Esau

GENESIS 27–28

Isaac and Rebekah had a set of twins. Their twins were both boys. They named the two boys Jacob and Esau. These twins were not identical twins as some twins are. Jacob and Esau were different looking and different acting. Each boy had a unique personality. Jacob was lovely to look at, rather thin and crafty. Esau was muscular, very freckled and hairy. Isaac and Rebekah were proud of their beautiful baby boys. Isaac took the burly freckled boy, Esau, and taught him to hunt for food with a bow and arrow. Rebekah took the more sensitive boy, Jacob, and taught him how to cook, how to manage a home with hospitality and grace.

The family might have had a wonderful life together. Isaac and Rebekah loved each other very much. But their lives became twisted and torn by the power of jealousy that rolled into their family relationships. Esau could plainly see how much his mother loved his brother. He saw how the women in the neighborhood fussed over Jacob's fine manners. The neighbors asked Jacob for advice when it came to home decorating and entertaining guests. Esau was not a well-mannered boy. He often forgot to use a fork when he was very hungry and gobbling a piece of roast. Jacob did not think he had everything he needed either. He resented the hugs and the good times that Esau had with their father. Jacob saw how the old man, Isaac, proudly patted the hairier and more muscular twin, introducing Esau to the men who gathered for special hunting events. Jacob's skin was far too delicate for camel back riding. He preferred reading books by the fireplace, rather than shooting arrows from a bow. Old Isaac hardly gave the time of day to his more sensitive, delicate son. Rebekah saw everything. She saw what Isaac did for Esau and she felt jealous for Jacob's sake. Isaac saw Jacob growing into a refined young man and he felt jealous for his son, Esau, who was not at all graceful around women or guests. As time went by each member of the family sat at the table during meal times and thought mean thoughts about the others. They spoke to each other with angry voices. Everyone wanted what the other member of the family had. Therefore no one in the family could be happy.

Isaac grew older and more feeble. He was lying on animal skins in his tent one day when he realized he would not be living much longer. So he called Esau to his side. "Son, I am old. I can no longer enjoy hunting in the forest or herding the sheep. I can no longer see as my old eyes grow blind. It is even hard for me to hear the song of the birds in the trees. Go out and hunt for a meal. Bring red meat to me and make a stew. Let's enjoy a meal together and then I will give you the gift of my blessing. You are my favored son." Esau went happily outside with his bow and arrows.

Rebekah had been standing outside the old man's tent. She knew how much a father's blessing meant to a son. To be the favored son and to receive a father's blessing was to receive a promise of peace and prosperity forever. Rebekah ran quickly to find her favored son, Jacob. The boy was polishing silver in the kitchen when she began to give him strict orders. "You must act now. Go out and get two young goats from your father's herd. Be quick about it! I will prepare a wonderful red meat stew with the goat meat and you will take the stew in to eat with your father in his tent. You must be the one to receive your father's blessing before he dies."

Jacob did not mind receiving a blessing. But he thought about this idea and asked a few questions. "What if my father notices that I am not the son he has chosen to bless? I might be cursed forever if I'm caught in this dishonest scheme." By this question we can tell that Jacob still had a conscience. He recognized the difference between right and wrong.

Rebekah had an answer for him. "You must make sure that your father does not catch you in this lie. You will wear one of your brother's robes into the tent with your father. You will cover your hands, your face, and your legs with the fur of the goats we kill for today's stew. The fur and the smell of your brother's robe will fool the old man. He is nearly blind now. Do not worry, but hurry. We do not have a minute to waste before that Esau returns and robs you of this important blessing."

When the stew was hot and rich with flavor, Jacob carried it with his fur-covered hands into the old man's tent. Isaac sat up in his bed and peered into the candlelit shadows. "Is that you, Esau? How did you get back so quickly?"

Jacob said, "God was with me in the hunt and gave me speedy success."

Isaac sat up as straight as his old crooked back would let him. "Are you my son, Esau? You have the voice of my son, Jacob." Jacob could hear his mother's cry of fear just outside the tent. "Come closer to me, that I might touch you and know that you are Esau." So Jacob moved closer to his father and the old man touched the goat's hair on the back of Jacob's hands. The old man sniffed the air and smelled the unwashed odor of Esau's robe.

"Phew-eee! It is, indeed, my favored son, Esau. Let's eat this stew together and then I will give you my blessing for your life."

And so the men ate together. When he was full the old man put aside his bowl and leaned toward his son. He said, "May God give you the dew of heaven, the fatness of the earth, and plenty of grain and wine. Let people serve you and nations bow down to you. Be master over your brothers. May any who curse you be cursed and may all who bless you be blessed." So Jacob received this blessing. Then he quickly gathered the dishes and left his father's tent. Rebekah clapped her hands with joy.

A few hours later Esau returned from his hunt with wild game in his pouch. He built a fire in the yard and began to cook what he had claimed as dinner from the forest. He carried the savory stew inside his father's tent. He was ready to talk, to tell wild and funny stories about his hunting adventures. But Isaac's question stopped him cold. "Who are you?" the old man asked his favored son.

"I am your favored son, Esau! You know me. I have come with the stew and you will give me your blessing for my life and for the lives of your descendants."

At this the old man began to tremble violently. His old bones rattled and shook with rage. "Who was it then that hunted game and brought it to me and I ate it all? Who was it that I blessed?"

"What!?" Esau was suddenly crazy with anger and grief. "If you have blessed another already, Father, bless me too!"

"Your blessing has been stolen. It is no longer mine to give," the father replied.

Both Isaac and Esau knew it was Jacob who had stolen the blessing. The more delicate twin had always been more deceitful too. Esau hated Jacob for robbing him of his birthright. Jacob hated his brother for knowing the darkness and dishonesty of Jacob's heart. No one sat down at the table together after that. Each member of the family took their plates and walked away to eat in separate places.

It was no longer safe for Jacob to be near Esau. Rebekah overheard Esau making plans to kill Jacob as soon as old Isaac passed away. Better a living son far away than a dead son in a grave close by. That's what the parents were thinking as they packed a travel bag for the more delicate and deceitful twin. So Rebekah and Isaac said good-bye to Jacob, sending him back to the land of their ancestors in Haran. "Find a wife for yourself there and make a life. We'll send postcards when we can."

So Jacob took the blessing he had stolen and left his family. He walked and walked and when night came he found a place under the moon and stars to lie down. He took a stone and put it under his head for a pillow. While the deceitful boy slept, he dreamed. Jacob saw in his dream a ladder that stretched from earth up into heaven. Angels were walking up and down the ladder. Going into heaven and coming out of heaven. God stood beside Jacob as he watched the angels coming and going. God spoke to Jacob saying, "This land that you are sleeping on will be your land. I will give it to you and to your children and to your children's children. I am with you. I will keep you. I will be with you wherever you go."

Jacob woke up and rubbed the sleep out of his eyes. "Surely, God is in this place and I did not even know it!" he exclaimed to the sky over his head. And then Jacob felt very afraid. He knew he was not an altogether good man. But God seemed to love and bless him anyway. Jacob looked to God that day and promised to pay attention to what was right and good for the rest of his life.

I'm going to remember this story of Jacob and Esau. It's a story that gives me much to think about. Sometimes people lie and play mean tricks on each other. Sometimes people steal. Jacob certainly was dishonest when he took the blessing that was intended for Esau. But even though Jacob had done things that were wrong, God's love for Jacob remained right with him. God kept blessing Jacob. That kind of love gave Jacob a chance to love and bless himself. Later, believe it or not, Jacob asked his brother to forgive him for what he had done. And you know? Esau forgave Jacob. The family finally had peace together, freedom from the ugliness of jealousy. God's never-changing love made it possible for all in the family to have what they needed. I'm going to ask you to help me remember how God blessed Jacob, the deceitful and more delicate twin. Are you going to help me remember?

The Show-off, Tattletail, Big-Headed Dreamer

GENESIS 37:1–36; 39:1–6; 41:46–47, 42:6

Once, a very long, long time ago there was a boy who had ten older brothers. They were all the sons of Jacob. The older brothers worked in the fields, herding sheep and sweating for long hours in the hot sun and dry air. The boy Joseph worked with his brothers in the field until the day he ran home and tattled on all ten of the older brothers, telling their father, Jacob, how they had tied all the sheep together with a rope and tied the rope to a tree while they napped on the ground. From that day on, it was not a good idea for Joseph to be out in the field with the older brothers. They had the tail of a wild beast just waiting to be tied to the seat of Joseph's pants.

Jacob loved Joseph more than he loved any of the other sons. Because this was true, the ten older brothers were jealous of Joseph. When their father, Jacob, made a fine coat of many colors with long sleeves for the favorite son, they were not at all happy. Joseph wore his fine coat because he liked it. But the older brothers believed he wore the coat to be a show-off. They spoke to the younger brother only when they really had to say something to him, like "Get out of my room!" or "None of your beeswax!"

You would think that this poor treatment from his brothers would cause Joseph to be sad or to feel some self-pity. And it might have done so if Joseph had been any less of a dreamer. He dreamed when he was snoring and he dreamed when he was awake. He dreamed early and he dreamed late. Joseph had a terrific imagination. And things might have gone better for him if he had kept his vivid dreams to himself. But Joseph felt the need to tell his brothers and his father about his dreams. "Listen to this dream that I had. There we were binding sheaves in the field. Suddenly my sheaf rose and stood upright; then your sheaves gathered around it, and bowed down to my sheaf." This made the brothers hate him worse than ever. Not only was he a show-off tattletail but their youngest brother was also suffering from a big head!

Joseph was off in his dreams and did not notice the anger of his brothers. That's why he did not hesitate, a few mornings later, as they were all eating their waffles and eggs, to report another dream. "The sun, the moon, and eleven stars were bowing down to me." The dreaming brother took a big bite of his waffle and chewed with much satisfaction while his father and brothers looked at each other and counted heads. "…eight, nine, ten, eleven!" Yes. That's right. There were exactly eleven of them, and all eleven had scowls on their faces as Joseph dreamed on…unaware that he was making enemies of his brothers. They were getting the idea that Joseph expected them to bow down to him. Even their father, Jacob, felt a little miffed at the idea that he might be in a position to bow down to his youngest son.

One day the older brothers were out in the field with the sheep and Jacob had an idea. He suggested to Joseph that the boy ought to do a good deed. "Take this cool water and sandwiches out to your brothers. Let them see how much you care." It was a very nice thought; you have to admit it. But the water and sandwiches were too little too late when it came to repairing the damage done to Joseph's relationship with his brothers. The older boys were watching their sheep when they caught sight of Joseph heading their way. They had time, as Joseph dreamily crossed the open field, to make plans.

"Here comes the daffy dreamer. Let's kill him. Throw him into a pit and say that a wild animal ate him. That's the end of his dreaming." But Reuben, one of the brothers, was not that cruel. He begged for mercy and to save Joseph's life.

Joseph met his brothers and their unleashed anger in the field. They stripped him of his many colored coat with its long sleeves and then they threw him into a deep pit and left him there. The ten older brothers ate the lunch that Joseph had delivered to them, feeling smug. It seemed like a good thing to have silenced the show-off, tattletail, big-headed dreamer.

While they were eating, the brothers saw a caravan of traders heading toward Egypt. That gave one of the brothers an idea. Judah said, "We could make some money if we sell the dreamer to the traders. We won't make a penny if we let him rot in that pit." The other brothers thought making money was a good idea. So when a group of Midianite traders passed by, the brothers sold Joseph to the traders for twenty pieces of silver. Then they waved to their father's favorite son as he was taken off in chains to Egypt.

Joseph was sold by the traders to Potiphar, one of the Pharoah's officials in Egypt. So Joseph lived in a palace and had many adventures, some good and some not so good.

While he was a slave in Potiphar's palace, Joseph grew much wiser. He was always a dreamer but he learned to use his dreams to help other people have better lives. It was one of Joseph's dreams that kept all the people of Egypt from starving to death during a seven-year famine. Joseph learned in his dream how to save enough food to save the lives of all the people of the land. Even Joseph's ten older brothers were forced by hunger to come to Egypt in search of food. They bowed down to this man of power in the palace, asking for food. They did not know that the ruler before them was their younger brother, their father's favorite son, Joseph. It was the show-off, tattletail, big-headed dreamer who shared grain with them and saved the family from starving to death.

You know, some people are pesky and difficult to live with. Sometimes we have trouble getting along with people in our very own family. But just because people are hard to live with does not mean they're useless. I want to remember that God was able to use that show-off, tattletail, big-headed dreamer Joseph for good purposes. Will you help me to remember that?

8

Baby in a Basket

EXODUS 1:1–14; 2:2–10

Joseph's brothers and their wives lived in Egypt and they lived very well. They had many children and their children had many children until the land of Egypt was filled with the family of Joseph, the Israelite people. There were so many of them that the king of Egypt grew nervous. "What if all these Israelite people get together and take power over the land of Egypt?" he asked his counselors. The new king did not know anything about Joseph. He only saw that his kingdom was filled with people who were not Egyptians. So that's why the Egyptian king decided to make slaves of the Israelites. He appointed taskmasters to force the family of Joseph to do hard work in the fields. They planted straw, harvested straw, and made bricks. Then they were forced to drag and carry the heavy bricks and great stones to build huge structures in the land of Egypt.

This was awful for the people of Israel. They were treated badly by the taskmasters, beaten and forced to work without enough water to drink or time to rest. Even so, the Israelite families continued to grow. More babies were born. The Egyptian king was worried. He was afraid that the enslaved people might become friends with some enemy of Egypt and assist in winning a war that would defeat the king's power over Egypt. So he said, "Every boy that is born to the Israelite families will be thrown into the Nile River." This was an awful thing for a king to demand. I know you would never demand such an awful thing, even if you were king or queen of a mighty land. But this king did not know you, so he did not know to ask you what was right and what was wrong.

One particular family in the people of Israel gave birth to a baby boy around the time of the king's awful demand. The mother looked at her wonderful baby and she knew that it was not right for him to be killed by the king's soldiers. So the mother hid her baby for three months while he was very small. But when he grew larger and his cries were louder, she could no longer hide him safely at home. The Egyptian soldiers were visiting the Israelite homes and listening for the sound of a baby's cry. So the loving mother made a huge basket out of papyrus reeds. She sealed the basket with pitch, which is like tar. When she saw that the basket she had made was a safe bed for her baby, she put him in it and placed the basket among the reeds on the bank of the Nile River. Then she instructed the baby's big sister, Miriam, to keep watch over the baby in his gently floating basket. Miriam hid in the reeds and watched.

Along came the daughter of the king! She was escorted by many women, women who assisted the princess in taking a bath in the river. Miriam watched the princess and her assistants coming close to the riverbank and close to the basket where the beautiful baby boy was hidden. Miriam was scared. When the baby whimpered and caught the attention of the princess, Miriam held her breath and waited. One of the women with the princess was ordered to go over and get the basket. The princess was curious about the sound she heard. Miriam watched the woman get her baby brother and his basket out of the reeds. The basket bobbed in the water while the king's daughter reached down and lifted the baby up into her arms. "What a beautiful baby!"

Miriam thought fast and made her move. She ran toward the princess and let her know that she thought the princess had very good taste in babies. "You are right, princess! That is a very beautiful baby. I think so too! I quite agree!"

"This must be one of the Israelite babies," the princess thought out loud. The royal woman cuddled the baby close to her heart when he started to cry. It was clear that she liked the baby very much.

That's when Miriam made her suggestion. "Would you like for me to get an Israelite woman to take good care of this baby for you? The princess looked into the baby's face and she wanted him to get very good care so she told Miriam to go quickly and find a woman who would be good to this baby and raise him to be wise and well. When Miriam returned to the riverbank with the baby's mother, the princess offered to pay the woman to take care of this child found floating in the water.

So it was that this baby boy was spared from the king's demand to kill all baby boys in the Israelite families. Miriam and her mother took good care of their baby, just as they would have done anyway. The baby grew strong and wise in his own home. When he was a young man they took him to the king's palace and offered him to the princess as her own son. She hugged the boy and looked into his face. Then she said, "I will name my son Moses because I drew him up and out of the water." (The name Moses means "drawn out of the water.")

He was drawn out of the water and taken into the palace where he lived as a member of the royal family. Each of us is drawn out of the water when we are baptized. God claims us, saves us from death, and adopts us into the royal family of God. Will you help me remember this baby named Moses? Help me remember Moses and this story every time we participate in a baptism.

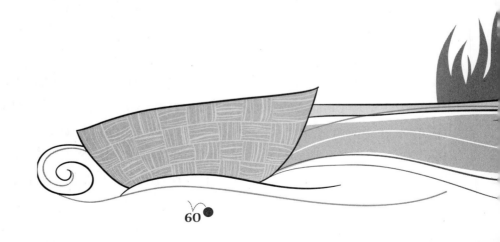

Escape From Egyptian Captivity

Exodus 2

Moses became a man and was married. He supported his family by working as a shepherd in the fields. It was while he was tending his sheep that he heard God's voice calling him. God said, "I am God. I spoke to Abraham, Isaac, and Jacob. I made promises to them long ago and I will keep my promises. I have seen how awfully the people of Israel are being treated by the Egyptians." Then God gave Moses the job of going to the Israelite slaves and telling them that God would soon be setting them free. So Moses went to the people of Israel and told them what God had said. But the poor slaves would not listen because they could not believe that anything could or would set them free from their difficult lives.

God had work to do, whether or not the Israelites believed he would do what he promised. He told Moses to go to the palace where he would tell Pharaoh, the king of Egypt, to let God's people go free from Pharaoh's land. Moses took his brother, Aaron, and went to the palace, where the brothers told Pharaoh what God had said. Pharaoh was not afraid of God and he liked having slaves to do so much of the hard work in Egypt. He did not want to let his slaves go free. He asked Moses and Aaron to perform a miracle since they claimed to be speaking for God. Aaron took his long shepherd's staff and threw it on the ground where it changed into a twisting snake! Pretty amazing, you say? Well, it did not impress the king of Egypt! Moses and his brother, Aaron, soon learned that this was old hat to the king. The magicians in his court could do the same trick. Pharaoh ordered Moses and Aaron out of his palace. He refused to listen.

God was not about to give up on the plan to set God's people free. Moses and Aaron received call after call from God, telling them to go back to the palace and let Pharaoh know that he was not strong enough to hold God's people in slavery when God wanted the people to be free. But Pharaoh's heart was hard and he would not listen.

God tried to get Pharaoh's attention. First there was the time when all the water in Egypt was turned into blood. Anyone who was thirsty and needed a drink had to drink thick, hot blood. It was very unsatisfactory. But Pharaoh did not want a drink of clear, cool water badly enough so that he would do the right thing. Moses came to him and said, "Let my people go!" For a minute, Pharaoh agreed to do so but then his heart hardened and he hollered, "No!" He would not let God's people go. So God filled the land of Egypt with frogs.

Everywhere people walked, they stepped on frogs. Frogs were in the soup and frogs were in the baby's bed. Frogs were in the road and frogs were on the table. It was awful but the hopping, plopping frogs did not soften Pharaoh's heart. Moses came to him and said, "Let my people go!" For a minute, Pharaoh agreed to do so but then his heart hardened and he hollered, "No!" He would not let God's people go.

So God sent swarms of gnats that crawled on every little thing and every big thing in the land of Egypt. It was awful having gnats on their lips and gnats on their sandwiches. Moses came to him and said, "Let my people go!" For a minute, Pharaoh agreed to do so but then his heart hardened and he hollered, "No!" He would not let God's people go. So God took the gnats away and covered the land with buzzing flies.

Flies sat on Pharaoh's nose and rubbed their feet together. Flies buzzed around the heads of everyone in Egypt until they all wanted to scream. And many of them did scream. "Take these awful flies away!" Moses came to Pharaoh and said, "Let my people go!" For a minute, Pharaoh agreed to do so but then his heart hardened and he hollered, "No!" He would not let God's people go.

God brought disease on Pharaoh's livestock so that all the sheep and cattle died in the fields. The entire land of Egypt smelled of rotting animals. Ugh! When this did not change Pharaoh's mind, God caused festering boils, nasty sores, to develop on the skin of the Egyptians. Pharaoh sat and scratched. Moses came to him and stood by the bathtub where the pharaoh soaked in salts. Moses said, "Let my people go!" For a minute, Pharaoh agreed to do so but then his heart hardened and he hollered, "No!" He would not let God's people go.

That's when God created a terrific thunderstorm and that storm brought huge hailstones to pound the Egyptians, their homes and their fields. Every tree in the land was broken down. But Pharaoh did not pay attention. He wanted to keep his slaves, the Israelites, right where they were. Moses came into the palace carrying a huge umbrella. Moses said, "Let my people go!" For a minute, Pharaoh agreed to do so but then his heart hardened and he hollered, "No!" He would not let God's people go.

So God sent Moses to warn Pharaoh of what was to come next. If Pharaoh would not let God's people go free, then a swarm of locusts would cover Egypt. There would be so many locusts on the land that no one could see the ground. The locusts came, as God had said, and they covered the land. They ate every single plant that the hail had not destroyed. All of these things were beginning to worry Pharaoh when Moses came to him and said, "Let my people go!" For a minute, Pharaoh agreed to do so but then his heart hardened and he hollered, "No!" He would not let God's people go.

Then God sent darkness to cover the land. No sunlight could be found. While the Israelites had light to go about their everyday business, the Egyptians were trapped because they could not see in the darkness. Moses came to him and said, "Let my people go!"

For a minute, Pharaoh agreed to do so but then his heart hardened and he hollered, "No!" He would not let God's people go.

That's when God sent the last and the most awful plague upon the Pharaoh and the Egyptian people. God told Moses what to expect. "Every firstborn son in the land, men and animals alike, will be killed. Every firstborn son—from Pharaoh's firstborn son to the firstborn sheep in the land of Egypt—all will die. But not one son will die among the Israelites. They will all be spared from the angel of death who will pass over the land of Egypt.

Moses and Aaron helped the people of Israel to prepare for the night of Passover when they would make their escape from slavery in Egypt. Lambs were killed and the blood of those lambs was smeared on the doors of the Israelite homes so that the angel of death would know not to stop there. No firstborn son or firstborn animal would die that night in the homes and the yards of God's people. Instead, while others were dying, God's people were being rescued.

Pharaoh sat up in bed at midnight and heard the terrible cries in his land as mothers across Egypt found their oldest sons dead and herdsmen found the oldest calves and lambs dead in their stalls. Even Pharaoh's hard heart was softened with grief when he saw his son dead in the bed. So Pharaoh called Moses and Aaron to the palace. The mighty man was trembling with sadness and fear. He had had enough. "I will let God's people go. Go quickly. Go away. Take God's people and leave this place!"

The people of God were ready. They had heard from God and

they knew this was the night they would be set free from slavery. They had been slaves for four hundred and thirty years. Now they were walking toward freedom at last! About six hundred thousand men and all the rest of their families hurried out of Egypt, running as fast as they could to be free.

Later that day when Pharaoh was no longer as shocked about the death of his son and the deaths of so many sons and animals in his land, the man's heart grew hard again. He wanted the slaves back where he had kept them. So he sent his army out to capture them and bring them back into slavery. The people of God were standing on the bank of the Red Sea when they saw Pharaoh's army thundering toward them. Their hearts filled with fear. There was no place to go! The river was in front of them and the awful army was behind them. Moses raised his voice in prayer and God heard the prayer of this man.

God was not scared at all. God had a plan. "Lift your staff and hold it up high," God instructed Moses. "Tell my people to move on, step forward, and the river will make a dry land for them to cross over."

And that is exactly what did happen! The people of God stepped with great faith into the river and the river was swept up and back out of their way, creating a dry path for them to walk over the riverbed with two walls of water at either side. It was amazing! Absolutely amazing! The people of God began to laugh and then they began to sing songs of praise. As they reached the other side they were playing their musical instruments and dancing together. They were free at last and standing safely on the other side of the river.

When Pharaoh's army got to the riverbank and rushed out between the walls of water that had been created as a way to move God's people into safety and freedom, God stopped the winds from blowing. And the walls of water fell crashing down into the riverbed, where Pharaoh's army drowned.

I'm going to try to remember that God would not give up on the fight to set God's people free. The love of God for the people of God is always at work, helping to move God's people toward safety and freedom. Will you help me remember?

10

The Battle of Jericho

Joshua 1–6

After Moses passed away, a man named Joshua became the leader of the Israelites. God told Joshua to be strong and courageous. God promised in return never to fail or forsake Joshua. So Joshua tried to get out of bed each day with hope in his heart. He had the power of God going before him. And Joshua trusted that power, teaching the people of Israel to trust in God's power every day and to act with strength and courage.

God had promised a certain area of land to the people of Israel, saying that the land beyond the River Jordan would belong to them. So it was Joshua who gave the army of Israel its orders as they marched to take the land that God had promised to them. The first challenge was to take control of a land called Jericho.

Joshua sent two spies ahead of the Israelite army, two brave men who went inside the gates of the city to see what the Israelite army would have to fight in order to take control of the land of Jericho. The spies went into the city and made friends with a woman named Rahab. When the king of Jericho found out that two Israelites were in her home, he sent orders to her, "Bring the men out." He intended to kill them before they could escape. But Rahab hid the two guests. Then she told the king," The men have just recently left the city. If you hurry you might catch them. Go! Go now!" The king and his men scurried out through the gates of the city.

Rahab went up on the roof of her house where she had the two spies covered with stalks of flax. Flax is a plant with thick stalks that can be spun into linen thread. Rahab had the flax on her roof where she had been working to make linen clothes for herself and her family. She bent down to whisper to the hidden guests under the pile of leaves and stems. "I know that you serve the true God of goodness and hope," she said. "I know how your God has given you victory after victory in other places as you have moved closer to us in Jericho. Word has come to us by way of travelers. Our hearts sank with fear when we learned you were in the plains close to us. I plead with you since I have dealt kindly with you. Deal kindly with me and my family. Give me a sign of good faith that you will spare the lives of my father and mother, my brothers and sisters, and all who belong to them."

The Israelite spies promised, "As you have been kind to us, we will be kind to you and to your family."

Then Rahab helped the Israelite spies to escape from the city. She put them both into a huge basket that she had made from flax stalk and she tied a rope to the basket so she could carefully lower the men down the outside wall of the city. She waved them away saying, "Go to the hills over there so that the king and his men will not find you. Hide for three days and then you will be safe."

The spies called up to her, "When we invade this land you must tie a red cord in the window of your home so we will know which house to save." They headed toward the hills and Rahab tied a red cord in her window on the outside wall of the city.

The spies returned to Joshua and the army of Israel on the third day. They reported, "Surely God is with us because the entire land of Jericho fears us."

Joshua gathered all the people of Israel on the banks of the River Jordan. The people relaxed there for three days. It was a time of rest so the people could save their strength for the battles ahead.

Then Joshua gave orders, letting the Israelites know what their work was to be in taking control of Jericho. "You are to walk together behind the Ark of the Covenant," he told them. (Now the Ark of the Covenant was the temple of God while the people of God were traveling and had no permanent home. Because they were on the road, they took the Ark with them. It was a long box with four carrying poles. It was where the people kept the stone tablets, the Ten Commandments from God, and where they believed God sat while they traveled. It was an honor and a great responsibility for appointed men to carry the Ark of the Covenant as the Israelites moved from place to place. The men who carried the Ark were priests, called Levites.) The people followed the Ark and the Levites to the Jordan River. As the nation of Israel crossed the Jordan River, God parted the waters and allowed them to go over on dry ground. The Levites stood in the center of the dry riverbed, holding the Ark of the Covenant, until all the people had crossed to the other side.

When everyone was on the riverbank, God told Joshua to select twelve men for the task of lifting twelve stones from the riverbed where the Levites had stood with the Ark of the Covenant. Those stones were stacked on the bank of the River Jordan and marked a sacred place as a memorial to the power and presence of God with the people of Israel.

When the priests reached the bank of the river with the Ark of the Covenant, the water of the River Jordan rushed back into its riverbed and resumed its mighty flow. The Israelite people marched on with strength and courage. The gates of Jericho were shut tightly. The king of Jericho had received word that the nation of Israel was coming to take control of Jericho. God said to Joshua, "You and all the people of Israel must march around the walls of Jericho. You must march around the city each day for six days. Everyone will walk together, all the women, children, and armies of Israel. On the seventh day you will circle the city seven times while the priests blow their trumpets. When they make a long and loud blast with the ram's horn all the people will begin to shout with a great shout and the walls of the city will fall down!"

So Joshua directed the march around the walls of Jericho daily for six days. Walk, walk, walk. Around the walls, every man, woman, brother, sister, and baby. Walk, walk, walk. The walls stood tall and strong beside them. On the seventh day they were so excited that they could hardly keep themselves from running. Could it be true, what God had said? Would the walls fall when they gave a shout? Walk, walk, walk. Then came the blast of the ram's horn followed by the trumpets. The people of Israel opened their mouths and shouted. Every girl and boy, every baby in mother's arms, every man, and every woman. They shouted! And the walls came tumbling down, as if made of straw, the walls fell down. Crashing, tumbling to the ground! And the nation of Jericho was conquered by the nation of Israel.

Rahab and her family were protected and honored just as she had been promised by the two spies. Joshua led the people of Israel into their new land and his fame as a leader and a man of God spread around the world.

I hope you will remember this story of Joshua and the walls of Jericho falling down. There's a song, a spiritual, called "Joshua Fit the Battle of Jericho." It goes like this...*[Story teller, sing a little of the song and give the children a chance to sing along.]* I hope you will remember the strength and courage of Joshua and the Israelite people. Theirs is a war story. And the war was won with a shout by God's people.

11

Samson Tells All

JUDGES 13–16

A very long, long time ago in the land of Judah, there lived a man and woman who received a message from God that they would be having a baby. The angel from God told the woman that her baby would be a son and he must never cut his hair. The long hair, the angel of God explained, would be the secret of his strength. He would grow up to be very strong and he would help to save the people of Judah from the Philistines, the enemy of the people of Judah. When the boy was born they named him Samson. He grew strong and God blessed him. His hair grew longer and longer.

Now Samson did some wild and crazy things with his great strength while he was a young man. Once while he was walking with his parents to Timnah, a lion roared at him. Samson killed the lion as if it were no challenge for him. Later, he walked by the carcass of the lion he had killed and found a swarm of bees and honey inside the lion's carcass. Samson reached inside the lion and scooped out much sweet honey. He shared it with his parents. Samson's hair grew longer and longer.

He grew to be a warrior, focused on fighting against the Philistines. When the Philistine army came rushing toward Samson, the spirit of God came upon him and his strength was tremendous. He reached to the ground and picked up the jawbone of a donkey. Using that bone as a weapon, he killed a thousand men. At the battle's end, he was very thirsty and asked God for a drink. A rock broke open and became a fountain of clear, cool water. Samson drank from it and was refreshed. Samson's hair grew longer and longer.

Samson traveled to the city of Gaza where jealous men heard of his tremendous strength and waited for a chance to challenge him. They hid in the dark, thinking that when Samson got up in the morning, they would attack him. But Samson slept only until midnight. He got up in the dark and walked to the gates of the city, pulled the gates down, lifted the main posts out of the ground and carried them on his shoulders to the top of a hill. The Gaza men who had planned to attack Samson were so astonished, they stood perfectly still. Samson's hair grew longer and longer.

Then Samson fell in love with a woman in the valley of Sorek. Her name was Delilah. The military leaders of the Philistines came to her in secret and asked her to discover the secret of Samson's great strength. They promised to give her eleven hundred pieces of silver if she coaxed the secret from him. Delilah liked the promise of money better than she liked Samson, so she started trying to coax the secret from Samson.

"Please tell me what makes your strength so great and how you could be bound so that you could be subdued by others," she begged.

Samson said, "If I were bound with seven bow strings, then I would be as weak as anyone." Samson's hair was growing longer and longer.

The Philistines gave Delilah seven bow strings and after Samson fell to sleep that night, she tied him up. The Philistines were lying in wait to attack the weakened man from Judah. "The Philistines are upon you, Samson!" Delilah shrieked to wake him. And Samson snapped the seven bow strings as if they were made of paper. Delilah pouted at this joke Samson had played on her. "Please tell me how you could be bound."

Samson said, "If you braid my hair and make it tight, then I shall become weak and be like anyone else." Samson's hair was growing longer and longer.

So while Samson slept, Delilah took his long hair and braided it tightly. Then she shrieked, "The Philistines are upon you, Samson!" The man awoke and unbraided his hair, laughing at Delilah. The woman pouted at his laughter. "If you truly loved me, you would tell me how you can be bound."

This touched Samson, for he did love Delilah very much, and so he said, "My hair has never been cut, not from the day of my birth. If it were cut, then my strength would leave me and I would be like anyone else." Samson's hair was growing longer and longer.

Delilah could tell that this was the truth. She waited until Samson went to sleep and then she went to the Philistines to collect her money. She returned to where Samson was sleeping. The woman put his head on her lap while she shaved off the long hair. He began to weaken immediately. "The Philistines are upon you, Samson!" she shrieked. Samson awoke to find he had no strength to fight off the Philistines, who dragged him outside, made his eyes blind and threw him into prison. There Samson was forced to grind grain at the prison mill. He walked round and round the grinding stones, doing the work of a mule. While he worked, Samson's hair was growing longer and longer.

The Philistines had a big party after a while. They were celebrating that the strong man from Judah was no longer strong. While they were partying, someone suggested, "Why don't we get Samson out of his prison cell and make him entertain us?" So they brought the blind man up and he performed for them. The Philistines were having a very good time, making fun of the man whom they had once feared.

Samson asked the guard who was with him, "Let me feel the pillars that this house rests against, so I might lean against them." The guard took the blind man to the pillars and Samson put his hands on them. The house was full of people. A crowd of Philistines were on the roof, nearly three thousand of them. They were watching Samson, wanting the blind man to do something funny, when Samson began to pray.

"God, remember me and strengthen me again just this once so I might take revenge on the Philistines for the loss of my eyes." Then Samson began to press against the huge pillars that stabilized the house. He put his left hand on one pillar and his right hand on the other. He pushed with all of his strength. Sweat poured down his forehead and across his chest. "Let me die with the Philistines," he prayed to God. And the great house fell down around Samson and those who were tormenting him and holding him captive.

I'm going to try to remember this man, Samson. I'm going to remember that Samson caused his strength to disappear when he gave away the secret of his strength. Samson refused to accept that Delilah was really not a very good friend. I'll bet you could tell she was not to be trusted. We sometimes cannot see the things we do not want to see. Any of us might give away the strength that God has given us. God gives us gifts and strengths so that we can do good things with our lives. Will you help me remember to be careful with the strengths that belong to me?

Samuel Hears a Voice

1 SAMUEL 1:1–28; 3:1–21

A very long, long time ago there was a woman named Hannah who poured her soul out before God, asking for a child. She went to the temple and prayed regularly. She prayed while she walked home. She prayed while she cooked. She let God know every time she thought of it how much she would like to have a baby. She thought it would be the best gift in all the world, to be somebody's mother. Although God always hears our prayers, sometimes God does not give us what we ask for, because it is not the best answer to our prayers. But God gave Hannah a wonderful baby boy. She named him Samuel. She was deeply grateful to God.

Hannah waited until Samuel was three years old and then she took him to the temple. An old man, Eli, was there and he was the priest of the temple. He had sons of his own but his sons were no help to him. They were wild and misbehaved, doing things they knew were wrong. So Eli was happy to hear it when Hannah said, "I have come to give my child to God as a gift from my gratitude. He will live here in the temple and serve God by helping you." This was good news for the old man because he could no longer see very clearly, nor could he hear all that well. He needed help around the temple.

Hannah prayed a prayer of thanks and left Samuel in his new home. Each year she returned to the temple, bringing with her a linen robe she had made for her child.

One night Samuel was lying in his bed and old Eli was lying in his bed down the hallway when Samuel heard a voice calling his name. "Samuel! Samuel! Samuel!" The little boy was quick to hop up out of his bed, a candle in his hand as he ran down the hall. He ran through Eli's bedroom door without knocking and was pretty surprised to see that the old man was sound asleep! Samuel woke him. "Sir, you called me?"

"What!?" The old man was startled. "Call you? No! Can't you see I'm sleeping?!" Eli pulled the covers up and rolled over. "Go back to bed, boy."

Samuel did as he was told. But he sure wondered why Eli called him and then forgot about it so quickly.

Just as he was sinking into a nice sleep himself, Samuel heard the voice calling again. "Samuel! Samuel! Samuel!" Up he jumped. The boy ran down the hallway, not even taking a candle to light his way. "Yes, sir?"

The priest was snoring loudly but Samuel shook his shoulder. "What?" The old man could not believe the boy was waking him again. "Have you lost your mind, boy? Get back to bed!"

Because Samuel was such a very nice boy, he did not want to say anything ugly. But he was starting to feel frustrated! Why was the old man calling him and then acting as if he had not? It seemed late in the night for silly games! He sort of stomped back to his bed.

Then he heard it again. "Samuel! Samuel! Samuel!" As quick as lightning, the boy rushed to Eli's bedside. "I know you called me. What do you need?"

Eli looked at the boy's face. He saw what was happening. It had been many years since the voice of God had been heard in this temple. "Go back to bed, Samuel. And when you hear the voice again, sit up and say: 'Speak, Lord, for your servant is listening.'" So Samuel did as he was told.

Sure enough. You know what happened. "Samuel! Samuel! Samuel!" This time Samuel responded, "Speak, Lord, for your servant is listening." God explained that she was going to do something in Israel that would make both ears of anyone who heard it tingle. God was planning to punish the sons of Eli for their bad behavior. Samuel heard what God had to say.

The next morning when the sun came up, Samuel went to the doors of the temple and swung them open. Light and warmth poured inside. Samuel could feel the power of God's presence all around him and within him.

At breakfast, as the two were eating their oats and drinking goat's milk, Eli asked Samuel what God had said in the night. Samuel really did not want to tell Eli what God had said. Samuel wished that God had said something pleasant. But Eli warned the boy not to hide any truth from him. So Samuel told the whole truth to Eli that morning. Eli was not happy to hear that God was planning to punish his sons. "I appreciate your courage and your honesty, Samuel," the old man said. From that day on, Samuel told the truth to Eli.

Samuel was a little boy born to a mother who prayed. He was a little boy who was given as a gift of gratitude to the service of God. Samuel grew and became a man. All Israel knew that Samuel was a trustworthy prophet of God, a man who listened when God spoke. Will you help me remember?

13

David Is Chosen

1 SAMUEL 16:1–13

When Samuel the priest was an old man, God said to him, "Fill your horn with oil and pack your bags, for I am sending you to Jesse in Bethlehem. I have provided for myself a new king of Israel among Jesse's sons." Samuel was scared that the existing king of Israel, Saul, would be pretty enraged if he learned that Samuel was out anointing a new king. But God said she had all of that under control. So Samuel put on his walking shoes and headed for Bethlehem.

When Samuel got to Bethlehem the leaders of the city recognized him as the powerful priest and prophet of God. They were scared of what he might want from them. Samuel said, "I come in peace." And the city officials relaxed. Samuel said he had come to have a big barbeque and he had brought along a cow to be slaughtered. "God has commissioned me to anoint the next great king of Israel," Samuel explained, "right here in this place." The special guests at the feast were to be Jesse and his sons. And everybody, for miles around, was invited to come and claim a place at the table. So logs were stacked and a fire was begun while everyone prepared for this special event. Samuel stood by the fire and gave thanks to God while everyone else was making ready for the barbeque. Samuel thanked God for all good things, especially for giving us guidance and hope in our lives. The people were arranging tables, spreading tablecloths, and making sure the drinks were iced while Samuel prayed. All the people nodded their heads in agreement. They were grateful to God too. And they were busy preparing for this special barbeque that Samuel had announced.

Jesse arrived with his sons. Eliab was the oldest. He came and stood before Samuel and the old priest thought, "Surely God's anointed is now before God."

But God said to Samuel, "Do not look at his handsome face or his tall, muscular body. For I have rejected him. I do not see as people see; people look on the outward appearance, but I look on the heart."

Samuel was surprised that this young man was not to be king. He certainly looked like a king. But he turned to face the next son of Jesse, Abinadab. He had Abinadab walk back and forth in front of him. God said to Samuel, "This is not the one." Then Samuel had Shammah walk back and forth in front of him. Was this the new king God had chosen for Israel? God said definitely not. Jesse had seven of his sons walk back and forth in front of Samuel, waiting for God to select one of them as the chosen king.

But God did not select one of them.

Samuel smelled the good smell of barbeque rising in the air. He was feeling ready to eat. The good smell was making everyone's mouth water. But nobody could eat; the holy celebration could not begin until God's chosen king was anointed by Samuel. "Are all your sons here?" Samuel wondered if Jesse had forgotten a son.

"There is one other son," Jesse was scratching his head with confusion. He was certain that his youngest son could not be chosen by God to be a king. David was out in the field tending sheep, where he played a small harp and wrote poetry. He was small for his age and he had a sweet face, not the kind of boy anyone would think of as a king. But Jesse sent for David because Samuel insisted and because Samuel said that nobody could sit down and eat until David stood before him.

Finally David arrived at the center of the city where everyone was gathered. Samuel looked at the shepherd boy, handsome with beautiful eyes. That's when God said, "Anoint him; for this is the one." Then Samuel took his horn of sacred oil and poured it over David's head, right in front of his tall and muscular brothers. The Spirit of God came upon David and rested there from that day forward. And David became the greatest king that Israel has ever known. To this day, all Israel looks forward to the crowning of another king as great as David. His reign has never been forgotten.

I'm going to try to remember that God chose the smallest and the least likely son of Jesse to be the greatest king of Israel's history. I'm going to try to remember that God looks, not on outer appearances, but on our hearts. Will you help me to remember?

14

David and the Giant

I SAMUEL 17

Long ago, in the days when the people of Israel had kings and queens, the Philistines gathered their armies for battle. Saul, the king of Israel, camped with his soldiers on a mountaintop across a valley from the mountaintop where the Philistines camped. Israelites. Philistines. Out of the Philistine camp stepped a huge giant whose name was Goliath. He towered over the tallest trees and picked his teeth with branches. He held a long spear made of shining bronze. He wore a bronze helmet so his face reflected the sun and the sound of his voice was terribly frightening to the Israelite men. The giant roared across the valley, "Ha! Ha! Ha! Little men, why have you come out for battle? You do not stand a chance! But since you are here, entertain me. Send a man out, your very best fighter, and let him challenge me. If your soldier defeats me in a contest then the Philistines will be your servants forever. But if I defeat the Israelite, then all of you must be servants of the Philistines. Ha! Ha! Ha! Come on, little men, who will it be? Which one of you dares to step forward and fight Goliath?"

The men of Israel shook in their boots and their knees went weak. Even King Saul felt great fear but he would never admit to it. After all, he was the king. So he took a deep breath and asked his soldiers, "Which one of you will spare the honor of Israel?" The king did not want his army to appear to be a bunch of wimps in the eyes of their enemy. Suddenly every soldier had work to do somewhere else. There were horses to be watered, tents to be set up, swords to be sharpened, boots to be polished, fish to be cooked. Not a single soldier stepped forward; not one of them wanted to fight Goliath.

David, the youngest son of Jesse, had three older brothers in Saul's army. David was young and he had the job of tending to the family sheep as they grazed on hillsides back home. He felt as if he were missing a great adventure while he tended the sheep and his brothers were away. Forty days passed and David could only imagine what his brothers were witnessing in battle. He prayed for their safety and victory over the Philistines.

Jesse was worried about his three oldest sons and after forty days he needed reassurance, some word from them that would give the father hope. So he packed wine, bread and cheeses. Then he directed his youngest son, David, saying, "Take these to your brothers. See how they are doing and bring back to me a sign."

David got out of bed the following morning before the rooster woke up. He startled the chickens as he dashed across the yard.

A neighbor promised to watch the family sheep while David went away. Because David was young and fast, it took almost no time at all for him to arrive at the camp where Saul's army was shouting a war cry.

"AAAYYYEEE!" The Israelite army stood facing the Philistine army. Then Goliath stepped out of the ranks and spoke to the Israelites again. David heard the voice and the giant's challenge.

The soldiers who stood around David did not notice the smaller boy as they spoke to one another. "Can you see how huge this Goliath is? The man who conquers him will certainly go down in history as a great hero. The king has promised that the man who kills this Goliath will marry the king's daughter and his family will be rich and free forever."

David drew himself up, squaring his shoulders and stretching upward to be as tall as he could possibly be. "Who," the shepherd boy yelled toward the army of Saul, "is this man who threatens the honor and lives of the Israelites? Who is this man who dares to defy the God of Israel by towering over the men of Israel?"

David's oldest brother heard the boy and was surprised to see him there in the military camp. "Go home, little brother! You are embarrassing me. Don't you see that many men, much braver and bigger than you, have the good sense to back away from the might of this giant?"

David shrugged his shoulders. "You have never have been able to see the power I pack in my young body, brother! You see me as a mere punk. And so I am. But I am also more than that. Open your eyes and I will show you the man I am becoming." David was beginning to feel that his hour to shine had arrived.

Soldiers went into the king's tent and told Saul what David was saying. Saul sent for the boy, who came and said to Saul, "Your fear can fly away for I am here, I will defeat this giant."

Saul looked closely at the boy before him, a young child with a shepherd's tunic and a shepherd's staff in his hand. David had thick curly hair and lovely olive skin, browned by days in the sun with the sheep. King Saul was deeply impressed by the enthusiasm and hope that leaped from David's eyes. "You are just a boy and this Goliath has been a mighty warrior for many years. He has built muscles for fighting and he has been trained to kill."

All the soldiers grew silent as the shepherd boy responded to the king. "I have kept sheep on the hillside for many years. Lions and bears creep over the hill, hoping to steal a lamb from the flock. How many times have I gone straight after a lion, striking it down with a stone from my sling, rescuing the lamb from the jaws of a lion? Too many times to tell, oh king. I am your servant, a shepherd who has protected his sheep from lions and bears. I will now act as your servant and protect the nation of Israel by striking down this giant."

The soldiers surrounding the boy could hold their silence no longer. First there was a single sniff, and then a giggle followed. Suddenly the whole army roared with laughter. They fell on the ground and rolled around laughing at the idea of this little boy killing Goliath in one-to-one battle.

The king held his arm up for the men to be quiet. "Prepare this soldier for battle!" he commanded.

David stood tall as if he had not even heard the laughter of the soldiers. Confidently he said, "God, who saved me many times from the lion's jaws, will also save me from the hand of this Philistine." Nobody laughed.

Saul gave David his own battle garments, his helmet and a coat of mail. The king gave David his sword. The boy tried to take a step forward but he could hardly move while wearing the king's garments and holding the great battle weapons. In fact, the boy was lost under the helmet and the coat of mail. "I cannot walk with these; this is not what I am used to wearing when I fight." David asked that the king's armor be lifted from his body. Then David took his shepherd's staff in his hand and he went down to the riverbank where he carefully selected five smooth stones. He put the stones in a pouch that hung over his shoulder and down his back. Then David walked straight toward the giant.

When the giant stepped forward and saw with his own eyes the boy who had come to fight, Goliath despised the boy. "Am I a dog that you come at me to fight with sticks?" David walked bravely along, holding his shepherd's staff in his hand. The giant snorted with fury. ""Come on then, baby brother, I will feed your flesh to the birds and the beasts of the field."

"You come to me with sword and spear and javelin," David roared back at the giant, "but I come to you in the name of the Lord of hosts, the God of Israel whom you have defied. This very day the Lord will deliver you into my hand and I will strike you down. For this battle belongs to God." Then David started running at the giant. He could hear his own little heart pounding with each step as his feet hit the ground. The boy put his hand in his bag, drew out a smooth stone, dropped it into his sling and slung it so that the stone hit the giant right in the middle of his forehead. The giant fell flat on his back with a thud that shook the earth. He was killed by a massive brain concussion.

A shepherd boy killed the giant and won the victory for Israel. David's ability to trust God was a secret weapon and it overwhelmed the giant, Goliath. The king and all of his army had been frightened and baffled by the giant. But David knew that the battle belonged to God and that God can win a battle with only a boy, a stone, and a sling.

Will you help me to remember this story of great faith? Will you help all of us to remember that the battles belong to God? We can trust that God is beside us and prepared to use us when help is needed.

Healed in Jordan's Muddy Water

2 KINGS 5:1–19

A very long, long time ago there was a commander of Aram's army who was a great man. He was a favorite of the king of Aram because he and his company had won so many battles for the king. The commander's name was Naaman. Although Naaman was a mighty conquering warrior, he had an awful skin disease called leprosy. Leprosy makes skin look terribly white and dry. Over time the disease makes parts of the body fall off. The doctors in the land could not cure Naaman of his disease.

There was, in Naaman's home, a girl who had been kidnapped during a battle and taken as a servant for Naaman's wife. The girl was from Israel. She worshiped God and had been taught to respect the great prophets of God. She felt sorry for Naaman with his awful skin disease and she said to Naaman's wife, "If only your husband could see Elisha, the prophet of God in Israel; he would cure him of his leprosy."

So Naaman took this information to his king and asked for

permission to go to the land of the Israelites. The king was pleased to learn that a cure might be found for Naaman's disease. He said, "Let me write a letter to the king of Israel." So Naaman set out with his soldiers to see Elisha, taking with him silver, gold, and garments as gifts. He went straight to the king of Israel and gave to him the letter that his own king had sent.

The letter said, "When this letter reaches you, know that I have sent to you my servant Naaman that you might cure him of his leprosy." When the king of Israel read this letter, he was terribly upset. He was not a doctor, not a magician, not a miracle worker. How in the world would he cure this man of his leprosy? The king of Israel was scared that if he did not cure Naaman, the king of Aram might get mad and declare war on Israel. The king of Israel was so upset he ripped his clothes. Now do not ask me to explain why the king ripped his clothes; it was something that people did back then to show how upset they were. "Am I God, to give death or life, that this man sends word to me to cure this man of his leprosy?" It was a desperate moment.

But when the prophet Elisha was told that the king was in the palace ripping his clothes, he came to see what had upset the royal man. Elisha let the king and Naaman know that he could help. So Naaman went to Elisha's little country home, arriving out front with war horses, chariots, and a host of soldiers. Elisha was busy when the commander of Aram's army arrived, so the prophet sent a message out: "Go wash in the River Jordan seven times. Your flesh shall be restored and you shall be clean."

Naaman, you understand, might not have been a king but he thought very highly of himself. The idea that this prophet would send a message outside rather than coming to meet the commander in person angered Naaman. And the idea that a great military commander would go wash in that muddy, shallow Jordan River was ridiculous. Naaman had expected a grand ceremony when he was cured of his terrible disease. He got back in his chariot and started riding toward home in a rage. His servants cared about Naaman so they chased after him and tried to talk reasonably with him. "If this prophet had asked you to do something really difficult, wouldn't you be glad to do it? But what he asked you to do is very simple. Wash in the muddy water of the Jordan. Why don't you give it a try?" Well, although Naaman was a very proud man, he was not a very ignorant man. He chose to wash in the muddy water.

So Naaman went down to the Jordan River and took off his mighty military garments. He dipped himself, one, two, three, four, five, six, seven times in the muddy shallow river water. He did just what the man of God had told him to do. And his skin was restored like the skin of a young boy. And he was cured of his leprosy. From that day on the mighty military leader worshiped the God of the servant girl in his home. He said, "Now I know that the God of Israel is the only God."

I'm going to remember Naaman and how he was healed of his awful disease. I'm also going to remember the servant girl who was in his home. You remember her? Well, she's very important in this story. She cared enough to tell about her faith in God and her faith in God's prophets. Because she shared her faith, Naaman was cured and came to believe in the God who cured him. Will you help me remember?

16

Three Brothers with Funny Names

DANIEL 3:1–30

A very long, long time ago King Nebuchadnezzar of Babylon attacked Judah in the land where the Israelites lived and conquered the city of Jerusalem. He ordered his soldiers to capture the healthiest and best-educated young Israelite men. He planned to bring them to his court, feed them, train them, and put them to work around the palace. King Nebuchadnezzar was a foolish king who thought only of himself.

Time went by. The king got an idea. He made a golden statue that was very tall and very wide and he had it placed in an open field in Babylon. Then he called for all the satraps, the prefects, governors, counselors, treasurers, justices, magistrates, and all the officials of the provinces to attend a dedication of the golden statue in the field. While they were standing before it, the herald proclaimed, "You are commanded, O peoples, nations, and languages, that when you hear the sound of the horn, pipe, lyre, trigon, harp, drum, and entire musical ensemble, you are to fall down and worship the golden statue that King Nebuchadnezzar has set up. Whoever does not fall down and worship shall immediately be thrown into a furnace of blazing fire." That seemed clear enough to everyone in Babylon. They heard the horn; they fell to their knees. Simple way to keep from burning in a fiery furnace!

Now among the healthy, well-educated young Israelite boys who had come to Babylon as part of the captured crowd, there were three brothers with very funny names . . . Shadrach, Meshach, and Abednego. These brothers were faithful to the God of Israel, the God of their mothers and fathers, the God who was with them during this time of being held captive. They bowed down and worshiped only the God of Israel. To them, it seemed wrong to bow down and worship a golden statue made by the king.

There were Chaldeans in Babylonia who were jealous of the captured Israelite boys. The brothers were gaining the king's favor. King Nebuchadnezzar had placed the brothers in charge of important work in his kingdom. The Chaldeans were worried that they might not get enough of the king's favor if he gave very much of his favor to these healthy and well-educated brothers in the palace. So they went to King Nebuchadnezzar and asked, "You, O king, have made a decree that everyone who hears the sound of the horn, pipe, lyre, trigon, harp, drum, and entire musical ensemble shall fall down and worship the golden statue and whoever does not fall down and worship shall be thrown into a furnace of blazing fire.

"There are certain Jews whom you have appointed over the affairs of the province of Babylon, named Shadrach, Meshach, and Abednego. They are not minding you, O king. They are not falling down and worshiping the golden statue that you have set up." These Chaldeans were royal tattletails!

Well, King Nebuchadnezzar was just the kind of king to get all bent out of shape over this. He puffed up. He turned red. He turned purple. He twisted this way. He twisted that way. He ran around in circles. He jumped up and down. Then he screamed, "Get Shadrach, Meshach, and Abednego! Bring them to me at once!" And so it was that the three brothers were dragged into the throne room and made to stand before the king. "Is it true that you refuse to bow down to the golden statue that I have set up?" The three brothers said this was true. The king started to get all bent out of shape again but he pulled himself together to give the brothers another chance. "I am going to have the horn, pipe, lyre, trigon, horn, drum, and entire musical ensemble sound a note and you will bow down to the golden statue. Or else . . ."

Shadrach, Meshach, and Abednego answered the king. "O King Nebuchadnezzar, we have no need to present a defense to you in this matter. If our God whom we serve is able to deliver us from the furnace of blazing fire and out of your hand, O King, let him deliver us. But if not, then be it known to you, O King, that we will not serve your gods and we will not worship the golden statue that you have set up."

The king was so enraged that he could no longer be recognized as king. His face puffed up like a helium balloon and some people were afraid the king would pop. He was very angry! He ordered that the fiery furnace be heated up seven times hotter than usual and he called for the biggest and strongest guards to come quickly. The guards came and tied the brothers up so that they could not move their arms and legs. Shadrach, Meshach, and Abednego were hurled like logs into the blazing fire. This fire was so very hot that the guards who tossed the three brothers into it were instantly tossed backward and killed by the intensity of the flames.

King Nebuchadnezzar was seated in his royal viewing chair watching and waiting for the end of this fiery scene. But something shocked him. The king jumped to his feet because he saw something in the furnace that his eyes could not believe. He asked his counselors, "Did we not throw *three bound men* into the fire?" The counselors nodded in agreement. "Then why," the king asked in a squeaky frightened voice, "are there *four* men in that fire and all four of them are walking about freely, *unbound?* They do not appear to be hurt by the heat of the fire and the fourth man looks like a god." He hollered into the fire, "Shadrach, Meshach, Abednego, come out!" So the brothers, leaving their mysterious fourth partner behind, stepped out of the furnace and looked around at the satraps, prefects, governors, counselors, treasurers, justices, magistrates, and all the officials of the provinces who were assembled to watch them burn. The brothers smiled sweetly. There was not a hair on their heads that was burned. Their tunics did not smell like smoke. The ropes that had bound them were gone. The fire had no power over these brothers with their strange names.

King Nebuchadnezzar said, "Blessed be the God of Shadrach, Meshach, and Abednego, who has sent an angel to protect them in the fire!" After that, the king insisted that the God of Israel be worshiped in Babylon and he gave the three healthy and well-educated brothers a big promotion in his palace.

I'm going to try to remember the great faith these brothers had in their God. I'm going to remember that when they held fast to their faith, they were able to change the faith of a king. And the king changed the faith of the nation. Will you help me remember?

Daniel Sleeps with the Lions
DANIEL 6:1-24

In the land of Babylon, there was a young man named Daniel, held captive after he was kidnapped from his homeland of Israel. Daniel found favor with royalty (the king and those in power) in the land where he was held captive. Daniel was a very good man. He ate his broccoli, spinach, and carrots, which made him very healthy. He did his work well and pleased his superiors. He had an excellent spirit. The Babylonians had a new king, King Darius, since King Nebuchadnezzar and his son, Belshazzar, had both died. King Darius promoted Daniel to a position of president over several satraps, giving Daniel authority to protect the king's interests in the kingdom. Because Daniel was so good and so favored by the king, there were men who looked for ways to destroy his life. The men were jealous and they did not like it that an Israelite slave had been given so much power over them.

The jealous men had a meeting and planned to find something bad to report to the king about Daniel. They hid in the bushes and watched Daniel as he came and went from home. They sat up in the trees and spied on Daniel through the upstairs windows. They hid behind walls where Daniel worked and listened, hoping to hear Daniel say something ugly about the king. But Daniel was a very good man and there was nothing the jealous men could find that would cause him to lose favor with the king.

That's why the jealous men went to the king and bowed before him, saying, "O king Darius, all the presidents of the kingdom, the prefects and the satraps, the counselors and the governors are agreed that the king should establish an ordinance and enforce it, saying that whoever prays to anyone, divine or human, for thirty days except to you, O king, shall be thrown into a den of lions. Make this ordinance and make it so that it cannot be changed." Well, King Darius imagined all the people of the kingdom praying to him for thirty days and he liked the idea very much. It made him feel quite special. So he signed the ordinance.

Daniel knew about the ordinance. But that did not stop him from following his habit of going to his room, opening his upstairs window and kneeling to pray to the God of Israel three times each day. He knew that it was his close relationship with God that gave him such an excellent spirit. He looked toward Jerusalem and praised God three times each day. The jealous men were watching and waiting to see this. It was all part of their devious plan. They went straight to the king, reminding him that he had signed an ordinance that could not be changed. "All people are, by law, to pray only to you, or they will be thrown into the lions' den." The king said that it was so. Then the jealous men told the king that Daniel was seen praying to his God three times a day.

This upset the king. He truly cared for Daniel and he tried to find a way to spare the Israelite's life. But that night the jealous men insisted that the king abide by the law. So the king called for Daniel and had him thrown into the lion's den with the roaring hungry beasts pacing back and forth. "May your God whom you faithfully serve deliver you," the king said to Daniel just before the faithful man was dropped into the den. A great stone was rolled over the mouth of the den and the stone was sealed by the king.

Then the king went home to toss and turn restlessly all night long. This was a very bad situation. The king began to pray in the night and he did not pray to himself. He knew there was nothing that he could do to save Daniel. He hoped that Daniel's God could keep the faithful man from being eaten by the lions during the night.

As soon as the sun came up, the king jumped out of bed and ran outside to lean over the mouth of the lion's den. "Daniel! Daniel! Has your God saved you from being eaten by the lions?"

Daniel hollered from down below, "Do not worry! God sent an angel who shut the lions' mouths so they would not eat me." The king was very happy to hear this and he ordered that Daniel be lifted out of the lions' den. There was not a scratch on Daniel after his night with the lions. Then the king ordered that the jealous men be brought to him and thrown into the lions' den. The lions, hungry and irritable after having their mouths closed all night long, jumped on the jealous men and ate them up.

I'm going to try to remember Daniel. I want to remember that even though he was very good and did nothing wrong, there were bad things that happened to him. He had trouble but it was not because he created trouble. I want to remember that the God he served faithfully was able to save him from being eaten by the lions. Will you help me remember?

18

Man Overboard

JONAH 1:1–17; 2:1–10; 3:1–10

A very long, long time ago there was a man who heard God's voice. The man's name was Jonah and God was calling him to go to the city of Ninevah. God asked Jonah to go to the big city and tell the people that they were not behaving well. God wanted them to change their ways. This did not sound like much fun to Jonah so he decided to run away from God. He ran down to the beach and saw a boat that was sailing for Tarshish. That sounded good enough to Jonah, so he got on board and went below deck to take a nap. It's very tiring to run away from God. Soon Jonah was snoring deeply.

God wanted to wake Jonah from his nap so God hurled a huge storm on the sea. The wind hit the water and raised great waves up in the air. The ship went up and then it crashed down. The crew on board the ship was fighting to stay on the boat and out of the sea. They were scared half to death. So they threw some of their load overboard, hoping to lighten the ship. The captain went below deck and asked Jonah what he thought he was doing. "Why are you taking a nap when the rest of us are fighting for our lives? Come help us!"

The sailors decided to draw straws, in the hope of learning which one of them had created this disaster. They were thinking that somebody must have made God mad! Guess who drew the short straw? You're right! It was that sleepyhead Jonah. The sailors stared at him with wide eyes. "What have you done? Where are you from? Who are you?" Jonah told them that he was from the Hebrew people and that he worshiped the God of heaven who made the land and sea. The sailors grabbed hold of anything they could to keep from being washed off the deck. They knew they were in big trouble because Jonah told them he was running away from God.

Pretty soon the sailors grew weary of holding on for dear life and they asked Jonah if he had any ideas. He said, "Just throw me overboard." Well, the sailors were not mean men. They hated to go home and tell their wives and children that they had thrown a man into the ocean that day. But the wind was harder and the waves were higher and they were getting exhausted. So they heaved Jonah into the water.

Over and over, down and down. Jonah blubbed deeper and deeper into the sea and then…all of a sudden…a huge fish came swimming by. The fish opened its mouth and water gushed in along with some algae and one flapping Jonah! The man went sailing by the sharp teeth, right past the tongue, and slid pretty as you please by the uvula. Then he was plunked into the belly of the great fish. It smelled awful in there. Jonah lit a candle and looked around. It was not a very pretty sight. And then you know what he did? This runaway preacher knelt down in the nasty gook inside the fish belly and he prayed. Now this prayer was not ordinary. But then, neither was this adventure very ordinary. Jonah prayed a prayer so pretty that it is written in the Bible. And God heard Jonah's prayer.

God spoke to the fish and the fish vomited. This sent Jonah flying through the air, up, up, up, and down, down, down, onto the sandy beach. Bump! He rolled over and over. Seaweed and sand filled his mouth. Jonah sat up spitting. God was there on the beach. "Are you ready to go to Ninevah?" God asked. I bet you know what Jonah said! He was scared *not* to be ready to go to Ninevah.

He brushed himself off and started walking to the big city. When he got there, it took him three days to cross the entire city, hollering, "Forty days more and Ninevah shall be overthrown!" The people heard Jonah's short sermon and they listened. Even the officials of the city paid attention. They all prayed and asked God to forgive them for their bad behavior. They changed the way they lived and God changed God's mind about destroying the city. Jonah's ministry in Ninevah was a complete success.

I'm going to try to remember Jonah. Sometimes I hear God calling me to do things I would rather not do. Sometimes I hear God calling me to go places I would rather not go. Sometimes I hear God calling me to say things I would rather not say. But I can tell by hearing Jonah's story that God has a way of getting our attention and helping us go in the right direction. Will you help me remember?

19

Up on the Roof

MATTHEW 9:2–8; MARK 2:1–12; LUKE 5:17–26

Jesus went to Caperneum for a while. When the people of Caperneum heard that Jesus was in town, they dropped everything they were doing and went to the house where he was staying. People filled the house and hung out the windows. People filled the yard and some of them climbed up in trees to get a look at Jesus. People stood out on the road and hoped for a chance to get closer to the man they had heard was able to heal the sick.

There was a man in Caperneum who was paralyzed. He could not stand on his legs and he could not walk. He had a mat on which he spent his days, always having to wait for others to get the things he needed. He was a nice man and people loved him. His friends wished he could be free to walk about, even to run if he wanted to. Four of his friends got together and planned to carry the man on his mat to see Jesus. Each friend took a corner of the mat and they hurried down the road to the house where Jesus was staying.

When they got close to the house they were stopped by the crowd. "Please, let us get closer to Jesus," the friends begged people as they pushed and shoved. "We want our friend to be healed." Slowly people moved to the side and allowed the four friends to carry the man on the mat closer to the house.

They could not get inside, even when they stood at the front door. It was far too crowded inside the house for four men plus one on a mat to enter.

It might have ended sadly but the four friends got a very good idea. One friend discovered a staircase at the back of the house. The stairs went up to a flat roof over the house. Why fight the crowd? The four friends took hold of the mat and carried the man up on the roof. Then they began to dig a hole in the roof! A hole in the roof! It was a very hot day and they grew so tired before the hole was big enough for lowering their paralyzed friend down to where Jesus was standing.

Jesus was telling a story inside the house. He looked up just in time to see a man on a mat coming toward him from the roof. Even Jesus was surprised! He looked up at the four friends who were peering down at him from the hole in the roof. Jesus could see for himself how much the friends loved this man. He could see in their faces that they had much faith. The four men believed that Jesus could heal their friend. They believed Jesus could give him the power to walk and run. So Jesus touched the man on the mat and told him to stand, roll up his mat, and walk. And the man was no longer a paralyzed man. He stood, rolled up his mat, and turned to walk. But the crowd was all around him. It was an amazed crowd. Somebody said, "We have never seen anything like this." Then they made a way for the man to walk through and to meet his friends in the front yard. I don't know for sure, but I'll bet that man skipped, ran, and hollered for joy all the way home!

I'm going to try to remember this story. I'm going to remember what a difference it made for these four friends to carry their friend to see Jesus. Will you help me remember these wonderful friends?

19

Feeding a Crowd

MATTHEW 14:13–21; MARK 6:30–44; LUKE 9:10–11; JOHN 6:1–14

Jesus and the people who traveled with him were tired. They had been busy listening to people's stories, healing people, and talking about the love of God. They needed rest. So Jesus suggested that they go on a mini vacation. "Let's get away to a private place all by ourselves," he said. "We'll relax for a while." So the men and women who were Jesus' closest companions got on a boat and rowed over the water to a distant shore. They expected some peace and quiet.

A crowd of people saw Jesus getting out of the boat on the other side of the sea. The crowd had come to see Jesus, to hear his stories of love and hope, to be touched by him, to be healed. They did not know that Jesus was tired. They only knew how much they wanted to be near him and to receive the blessings he had given to others. People were calling him a "miracle worker." He seemed to love and care for everyone. Nobody wanted to miss a chance to see him up close. So the crowd hurried around the shoreline and pressed in around Jesus and the disciples. There seemed to be little chance that the tired group could get a mini vacation.

Jesus looked at the crowd of people surrounding him and he loved them. He understood how much they wanted miracles in their lives, how much it meant to them to meet someone who loved them just as they were. No one felt the need to put on fancy clothes when they met Jesus. People did not feel that they should be prettier, any smarter or different than they were as ordinary, every day people. Jesus brought out the best in every one. He began to tell them stories, helping the people who stood in front of him to see the good in themselves and to see the good in others. He taught them how to treat one another with respect by the way he treated everyone with respect. People were learning so many important things from Jesus that they forgot about going home. They forgot about needing to prepare a meal. They wanted more of the love and hope that Jesus was giving away for free.

The sun was sinking lower in the sky and the disciples of Jesus grew worried. One of them, Peter, went to Jesus and interrupted his teaching. "Jesus," he said, "it is getting late. This crowd needs to go home and get dinner. I know I'm hungry and I want to catch a few fish for myself and fry them." Peter's mouth was watering as he thought about the taste of salty fried fish. "Let's tell this crowd to go into town and buy some food for themselves."

You could have knocked Peter over with a feather when Jesus surprised him with this response, "*You* give them something to eat."

"What?!" Peter squeaked. "Me? Surely you are joking, Jesus. Even if there were a McDonald's or Wendy's across the hill there, I do not have enough money to buy a burger for every single person in this crowd. Why there must be at least five thousand men here and that's not counting all the women and children in this crowd!. How could I afford to feed them all?!" The other disciples of Jesus were coming closer to hear this conversation. It was astonishing for Jesus to say that Peter should feed this crowd.

Jesus was as cool as a cucumber, not one bit excited or worried. He looked around at the people in front of him and he wondered out loud, "How many loaves of bread are out there in the hands and pockets of these people?" The disciples sighed great big sighs. They could tell that this was one of those times when Jesus was going to teach them a lesson. They just hoped the lesson was over before they all starved to death out there on the seashore! They went walking among the crowd, asking first this man and then another woman, "Do you have a loaf of bread with you?"

John was the last disciple to come back to Jesus. "There is a girl in the crowd whose mother packed a very generous lunch for her. The child has a lunch pack with five loaves of bread and two fish. She will be satisfied this evening while the rest of us look on with growling stomachs."

Jesus called the little girl to come forward with her lunch. She was very happy to be called up front where Jesus stood. A big smile covered her face as Jesus looked at the loaves of bread and the fish. "Would you be willing to share this lunch?" Jesus knelt down so that he was no taller than the girl when he asked the question. There was absolutely no doubt about it. That little girl was very happy to share her food. She put it all, the bread on top of the fish, into Jesus' hands and waited to see what he would do with it. Jesus was amazed at her generosity and enthusiasm.

He told the crowd to sit down on the grassy hillside. "Divide up into small groups so you can enjoy getting to know each other." Jesus directed the crowd and then, when they were seated in small groups, he took the five loaves and two fish and he held them up in the air, as if offering the food to God. He asked God to bless the little girl's meal. Then he began to break the loaves and fish into pieces. He offered the little girl a huge hunk of wonderful soft bread and a big piece of salty fish. She was still smiling as if her happiness would never end.

The disciples came forward to help him serve the crowd. Basket after basket was filled with bread and fish. The groups of people were laughing and telling stories while they ate. Fish and bread. Fish and bread. Everyone was eating and no one had to worry about having enough food. The baskets remained full as long as the people were hungry. The people were stretched out on the grass, taking in the beauty of the setting sun. The disciples walked around picking up scraps and leftovers. They collected twelve baskets filled with leftovers. This made them absolutely speechless. It was a miracle. Five loaves of bread and two fish had fed an entire crowd!

I am going to try to remember that a huge crowd of people was fed when a little girl was willing to meet Jesus face to face and then share everything she had in her lunch pack. Will you help me remember?

20

Diana's Friendship

MATTHEW 19:13–15; MARK 10:13–16; LUKE 18:15–17

The sun was very hot that day but a refreshing breeze helped cool Diana as she walked quickly to keep up with her mother's fast pace. Diana was four years old and she was going to meet a man named Jesus. Her mother said that Jesus was a great teacher and that he could heal people. He was a holy man. Diana only knew that her mother wanted her to walk faster and she could tell that her mother was very excited about meeting this man. Her mother pointed straight ahead. "It's him!" Jesus was in the field, sitting on a rock under an olive tree. Diana could see crowds of people coming through the field from every direction. "Hurry, Diana!" her mother pulled on her arm and walked faster.

People were tightly packed around Jesus when Diana and her mother got close. "You're small, Diana. Crawl between people's legs and get close to him. Ask Jesus for a blessing for you and for me." Diana got down on the ground and crawled toward the front of the crowd. It wasn't easy but she made it to the front and stood up straight. She was just about to dash toward Jesus when a very tall man with thick black hair and a bushy beard scowled at her darkly. "Get back!" He swatted at Diana. She ducked and turned to crawl quickly back through the forest of legs.

But another voice spoke. "Wait! Don't go away!" Diana peered over her shoulder and saw that Jesus was looking right at her as he spoke. She stood up and turned toward him as he spoke to the tall man with the beard and scowl. "Don't swat at children and don't keep children from coming to me." He stretched his arms out widely and motioned for Diana to come to him. Pulling her up on his lap, Jesus looked at the crowd of people and said, "Always allow children to come to me and watch the way they come. They are trusting, ready to love and to be loved. Theirs is the way to enter the kingdom of God." Diana had no idea what Jesus was talking about and really she didn't care. She was feeling so safe and warm in his lap. She kept sitting there while Jesus went on talking to the gathered crowd. When she got down from his lap and headed for home with her mother, Jesus called to her, "Diana, you are my friend. Go in peace." It was the blessing Diana's mother had asked for. They went home feeling peaceful.

It was one year later when Diana's mother announced that Jesus would be coming by again. He was on his way to Jerusalem. Diana knew nothing about the Bible or a cross. She had never heard about Easter. Never had she dyed eggs or looked for colorful eggs in hidden places. Diana lived nearly two thousand years ago. She only knew that she was going, once more, to see

Jesus. This time she hurried with her mother. She was eager to see her friend.

When they got to the gates of Jerusalem, Diana could see a crowd beside the road. People were waving palm branches and scarves. They were shouting, "Hosanna! Hosanna!" Diana picked up a palm branch as she ran and she waved it high in the air. Jesus was coming and he was riding on the back of a donkey. Diana took the scarf off her hair and waved it in the air with her palm branch. "Jesus! Look, it's me! Diana! I'm over here!"

Jesus was riding closer and closer until he was right beside the little girl as she shouted. His body was close but Diana could tell that the thoughts of Jesus were far away. Diana was surprised to see how sad Jesus looked. Just as she was noticing his sad face, Jesus noticed her and he lifted his hand in a greeting. Diana saw a big tear roll from his eye and slide down his cheek. Diana's heart was breaking. What was it that made her friend so sad? "Jesus!" she called out, her voice clear and loud, "You are my friend. Go in peace." As she returned this blessing to her friend, she threw her palm branch and her scarf on the dusty road in front of the donkey. Jesus rode on into the city of Jerusalem.

I am going to remember that my friends need me as much as I need them. Diana blessed Jesus when he really needed a blessing. We can all bless each other with understanding and offering words of kindness. Even Jesus needs good friends the same way we need good friends. I am going to try to remember that. Will you help me remember?

21

Healed by Jesus

MARK 5:21–43

A nice refreshing breeze was blowing off the sea while a crowd gathered around Jesus. This was a long time ago but it's still so real to those of us who follow Jesus today. He was talking with the crowd of people gathered around him when a man named Jairus came rushing to his side. The man was a leader at the synagogue. He fell down before Jesus and begged, "My little daughter is very sick! I'm afraid she might die. If you would come to my house and touch her, she would be made well and she would live." Jesus told Jairus to show him the way to his house. And Jesus followed the father.

A woman was following in the crowd that day. It was a very courageous thing for her to be out in the crowd. The law said that a sick woman ought to stay inside and not come near others. For twelve years she had been sick and staying inside her house. Doctors had come to her house and they had not made her well. She had no money left after paying all the doctors for their house calls. But she was still sick. So the woman drew up all her courage and broke the law by coming out of her house and joining the crowd around Jesus. She pushed this way and then she pushed that way. She had heard stories from neighbors, stories about Jesus and how powerful his love could be. People were being healed by his loving touch. She finally got through the crowd of people and saw Jesus in front of her. He was facing the other way so she knelt down and reached toward his back. She touched the hem of his robe. That's all. She just touched the clothes that were touching him. And she knew instantly that she was well. Her long sickness was ended.

Jesus stopped talking and walking. The crowd got quiet. Jesus looked around and asked, "Who touched my clothes?" This scared the poor woman half to death because she was scared she had done something wrong.

The disciples laughed at Jesus, saying, "Look at this crowd pressing in on you. How could we know which person touched your clothes?"

Jesus said, "I felt power pour out from my body."

The woman could not keep silent. "I touched you, Jesus. I was so tired of being sick."

Jesus loved her and was glad that the touch had healed her from her sickness. He said, "What great faith you have! And that faith has helped to make you well. Go in peace. You are healed."

Then he went on toward the home of Jairus. That's when some people came running up to Jairus and Jesus. They said,

"It's too late. We're so sorry. The little girl is dead." This really upset Jairus but Jesus touched him and said that they would go home and see for themselves. Jairus hoped that Jesus could do something wonderful.

When they got to the home of Jairus, people were standing around and many of them were crying. Jesus walked up to the front door and told the people that the little girl was not dead. Some of the people thought Jesus was crazy. Some of them thought he was cruel. Some of them were very curious about what he was going to do next.

Jesus took some of his disciples and went inside. They went to the little girl's room with her mother and daddy. Jesus took the hand of the child and said, "Little girl, get up." And she did! She got up and started showing Jesus some of her favorite things in her room, some of her artwork and puzzles, her books and her toys. Jesus was glad to see the things she treasured. Then he said, "Get this little girl something to eat." And so they all had sandwiches together. And maybe a cookie or two for everyone at the table.

I'm going to try to remember this story of Jesus and all the love in his touch. I'm going to remember the people who were healed by his touch. Will you help me remember?

22

Jesus Heals a Man

LUKE 5:12–16

Jesus was visiting some of his friends in the city, walking through the busy and crowded streets with them. The market was full of people who were buying and selling. Dust was flying up in the air as camels and oxen were slowly walking through the narrow streets. Jesus was looking at the fruits and vegetables that were displayed in the marketplace. He was hungry and thinking about lunch.

Suddenly a man ran to Jesus and threw himself at Jesus' feet. The man had skin that was a real problem for him. There were sores on his head, on his back, on his arms and legs. The sores itched and he had to scratch them. The places he had scratched were bloody and ugly. Other sore places on his body that were not bleeding were very dry, white, and flaky. From a distance, other people could see that this man had a disease called leprosy. The disease was so awful that his ears and a few of his fingers had fallen off. The disease had slowly eaten them away. Part of the man's nose was missing. He had been suffering with leprosy for many years. "Lord!" the man cried, "If you choose, you can make me clean!"

Jesus stopped walking and he stopped looking at fruits and vegetables. He even stopped thinking about how hungry he was. This man on his knees in front of him had to be a man with tremendous courage. Jesus knew the laws about leprosy. A person who had this awful disease was breaking the law to come into the marketplace. The laws of that time and culture said that a person with leprosy had to stay outside of town, away from people.

If the man with leprosy saw someone coming close to him, the law said that he had to shout loudly, "Unclean! Unclean!" It was a warning. It was a law intended to protect people from catching leprosy. The law left people who had the disease of leprosy all alone and lonely. The man with the awful disease was very close to Jesus, begging for help and Jesus knew that the man could be severely punished, even executed, for coming into the marketplace.

Jesus' heart was moved and tears filled his eyes. The man wanted so badly to live a normal life, to be free to go where he wanted to go. What an awful thing to have to shout "Unclean! Unclean" every time another person walked close to him. Jesus wanted the man to be rewarded for his faith and for his courage rather than to be punished for having a terrible disease he had not chosen for himself. Jesus reached out to touch the man and the friends who were with Jesus gasped in surprise. The friends thought that Jesus would catch the disease of leprosy if he touched the man. They were standing back, far away from Jesus and the man who waited on his knees at Jesus' feet.

The fact is this: it is very difficult to catch leprosy from another person. Even though leprosy is an awful disease it is not a disease that is easily spread from one person to another. In order to catch leprosy from someone else, we would need to live closely with that person over a long period of time, sharing the same bed with them, eating off one spoon with them, sharing a single toothbrush, and bathing in the same bathwater. Even then, a very healthy person might not catch leprosy. But the people around Jesus in the marketplace did not know any of this. They believed that leprosy was easily passed from one person to another. They felt great fear because the man with leprosy was so close to them. Looking at how ugly the man's skin was with white flakes and bloody sores, his nose half gone and his ears missing completely, some of the people in the marketplace were prepared to kill the sick man. Many people in the marketplace hated the man. They believed that he had the awful disease because he deserved it. People thought that leprosy was a punishment for not behaving well, for doing something that angered God.

Jesus could see more truth than the other people could see. He saw plainly how much the sick man wanted to be well. He saw how much the man loved himself and his life. Jesus could see great hope in the man's eyes. Jesus saw so much more than the disease when he looked at the man. Jesus saw an amazing person.

So Jesus reached out his hand and touched the man with leprosy. Jesus put his hand on the man's shoulder and said, "I choose to make you clean and whole." Jesus smiled as the white flaky skin disappeared and the itchy, bloody sores went away. The man's nose, fingers and ears were restored as he leaped to his feet. People in the marketplace were totally amazed. Could this be for real? The man who had leprosy was now a man among men just like any other man in the marketplace. Those who had their swords drawn to kill the man stood back. They had planned to kill a leper, a man who was breaking the law by bringing his illness into the marketplace. But now this was not a man with leprosy. He was a man healed and made whole. He was thrilled, leaping up high in the air and saying, "Thank you! Thank you! Thank you, Jesus!"

Jesus gave the man a long, tight hug when the healed man stopped hopping up and down. The man put his head on Jesus' shoulder and cried for a while. He was just so happy that he felt every feeling any of us are capable of feeling—all at the same time! The disciples of Jesus watched. They were just as amazed as anyone else. They had seen Jesus performing healing miracles before. But this was truly amazing. People went on their way that day, buying and selling fruits and vegetables. Jesus invited the man who had been sick to eat lunch with him and his friends. It was a good time and a good meal.

Some people went away from the marketplace that day wondering about Jesus and feeling afraid of his great love and power. Love and power like Jesus had could change things in the marketplace. Not everyone thought that Jesus was good. He had broken the law by reaching out to touch the man with leprosy and even though the man was now healed, there were some people in the marketplace who believed that Jesus should be arrested for breaking the law. But some people left the marketplace that day determined to be more loving and kind to all people no matter how they looked on the outside, no matter how much fear they felt about another person's disease. Some people had their eyes opened in the marketplace that day and they could see, like Jesus could see, something much more important in the man than a disease. They could see a beautiful human being with a great desire to be loved and touched, to live freely and joyfully.

Will you help me to remember this healing story? Will you help us, church people, to have eyes that see deeper truths? I hope we can be the kind of people that see how much all of us want to be loved and made whole.

The Good Neighbor

LUKE 10:25–37

Once there was a lawyer who came to Jesus with questions. "Teacher," he asked, "what must I do to live forever?"

Jesus looked at the lawyer and Jesus knew that the lawyer already knew the answer to his own question. The lawyer wanted to put Jesus in a position where Jesus said something wrong, something that would get Jesus into trouble with the religious authorities. Jesus was growing tired of the tricks. "What is written in the law? What do you already know about it?"

The lawyer answered, "You shall love the Lord your God with all your heart, and with all your soul, and with all your strength, and with all your mind; and your neighbor as yourself."

Jesus nodded. "That's the answer to your question." Then Jesus turned to walk away. But the lawyer stopped him with another question.

"And who is my neighbor? Who is it that I have to love as I love myself?"

Jesus sat down and motioned for the lawyer to have a seat beside him. Then Jesus told the man this story . . .

A man was taking a trip from St. Louis to Kansas City. He was driving a very old and worn-out car. It sputtered and backfired along the interstate highway. All the other cars sailed around it. The driver of the old car was making progress until one of the tires on his old car blew out. The man steered his car to the side of the road. Just as he was taking a spare tire and jack out of the trunk, he was attacked by robbers. Several mean men beat him up, took his wallet, and left him lying beside the road. The poor man was bleeding and moaning, unable to help himself.

A car slowed as it went by the poor man, who was half dead and half alive. A priest was driving the car. The priest looked at the man beside the road and he thought about helping him. But the priest had important people waiting for him in Kansas City. He could not be late to meet the important people. The priest put his foot on the gas and went on his way. The poor man moaned in pain and coughed in the dust.

Then another car came by and slowed as it passed the beaten man beside his old car with its flat tire. A preacher was driving the car. The preacher was all dressed up and on his way to Kansas City to meet with other preachers. He thought about helping the man by the road but he really had no time to stop the car. The preacher looked at his watch and then he put his foot on the gas. The car went by the wounded man in a flash. The poor man longed for a drink of water and he moaned.

Then another car came by. A Muslim man was driving the car. He slowed his car and saw that a person was lying beside the road. "Oh dear!" he thought. "This is awful!" He pulled over to the side and stopped his car. He carried a first aid kit in his glove compartment.

He took Neosporin ointment and some gauze with him as he walked back to the poor man. He bandaged the bleeding wounds and put a splint on the man's arm because it looked like it might be broken. Then he picked the man up and put him in his own car. He drove to the next town where he found a minor emergency clinic. He sat in the waiting room and read an old, wornout magazine while the stranger was treated by a nurse and a physician. Then the Muslim man took the man to a Holiday Inn Express and got a room for him. The poor man was so glad to lie down in a clean bed. He went to sleep immediately. The Muslim man covered him with the bedspread and quietly walked out of the room.

The Muslim man went to the desk and paid for the stranger's room. Then he said, "Here is another hundred dollars in cash. Use this for the man's food over the next two days. I will pass this way on my return trip. If the man needs anything, see that he gets it and if this amount of money does not cover his needs, I'll make up the difference."

That was the end of the story that Jesus told to the lawyer. Jesus looked at the lawyer and asked, "Who is the good neighbor in this story?"

The lawyer answered, "The one who had mercy."

Jesus stood up and shook the lawyer's hand. "You go on with your life and I ask you only to do like the good neighbor in this story. Have mercy on people you meet along the way."

Will you help me and all the people in your church to remember this story? Will you help us all to remember to have mercy on people, all people we meet along the way? Thank you.

The Extravagant Mother

LUKE 15:11–32

Once there was a mother and she had two daughters. The youngest daughter said to her mother, "Mom, give me all of the allowance you ever plan to give to me. Give me all the money you plan to spend on my college education. Give me whatever would be mine after you die. Give it to me now. I want to go out into the world and have adventures on my own."

So the mother gave the daughter what was hers and a few days later the younger daughter went away. She went into the city where she wandered through the malls filling shopping bag after shopping bag with all sorts of jewelry, bubble bath, shoes, and short skirts. She attended wild and crazy parties in the evening when she could no longer shop. She stayed in a fine hotel where the doorman saw her safely to her room each evening. She ate hot dogs, hamburgers, potato chips, and chocolate candy bars. She drank sodas from morning to night. What a wonderful adventure the youngest daughter had! She no longer needed her family or home!

And then her money ran out. The girl could no longer pay for her room at the hotel. She could no longer afford to shop. She had no money for hot dogs or hamburgers and nobody invited her to wild parties after her money ran out. The daughter started out in search of a life for herself. She walked along the highway outside of the town. That night she slept in the backseat of a wrecked car in a car junkyard. She ate Alpo with the junkyard dogs.

The girl sat among the piles of wrecked cars and wished for something good to eat, some place nice to sleep, and a friend who would stay by her side.

Finally her stomach could no longer stand to eat another bite of dog food. Her back was aching from the lumpy car seat she was using for a bed. The girl thought to herself, "I know that my mother has camping equipment in the storage shed out back of the house. I would be better off to sleep in a sleeping bag inside a canvas tent in my mother's backyard than to stay here and die of hunger. I'll go back home, apologize to my mother for how foolishly I have behaved, and I will ask if I can mow the lawn and trim the hedges in return for a sandwich, a cookie, and a soda." So the youngest daughter started walking toward home.

The mother was standing at the kitchen sink, drying dishes and wishing that all of her family was together and happy . . . when she saw her youngest daughter coming down the sidewalk from the end of the street! The mother threw her towel up in the air and ran outside on the porch to see her daughter more closely.

She waved her arms up in the air with a great gesture of joy. Tears of happiness filled the mother's eyes and she could stand still no longer. She began to run and as she ran her daughter began to run too. They ran right into each other's arms and hugged tightly while they cried. "Mother," the youngest daughter sobbed, "I've been foolish. I am sorry for wasting so much time and money. I want to come home. I will work. I will earn every meal that I eat."

The mother had something to say that could no longer wait. "I want to throw a party for you! I'll get the charcoal in the pit and we'll grill hamburgers and hot dogs. I'll order a cake from the bakery and buy six flavors of ice cream! We'll have punch that will knock your socks off!" The mother hugged her daughter tightly. "Because you were lost and now you are found, we need to have a huge celebration." The mother went into the house and put dance music on the CD player. Even the dog was kicking up her heels with joy.

Just then the older daughter came downstairs from her bedroom where she had been working on her algebra homework. "What's happening?" she asked, looking sternly at her mother. The older daughter was the serious type.

"Your sister was lost and now she is found! We're going to have a big celebration this very night!" the mother exclaimed. "I plan to order a bakery cake and I'm going to the grocery to buy six flavors of ice cream! Can I get anything for you while I'm there?"

But the older sister did not answer her mother. She puffed up with anger and jealousy, swelling into a rage. The mother stopped and looked closely at her oldest daughter. "Come on, now. You are not going to be angry about your sister's return, are you?" The mother reached out to hug her daughter. But the older daughter backed away from her mother's embrace.

"You listen to me, Mother." The daughter spit her words. "I keep my room clean and I save my money. I make good grades at school because I study hard and keep up with all my assignments. I feed the dog and empty the cat's litter box three times a week. But you have never ordered a bakery cake and gone to get six flavors of ice cream for me. Now this foolish sister of mine who wasted so much of your money and so much of her life has come crawling back here and you throw a big party! I am offended."

The mother sat down and took a deep breath. She loved her daughters more than any words could say. She wanted both of her daughters to understand that . . . "I love you all the time. Everything I have is yours all the time. But we have to throw a party for your sister. She was lost and now she is found."

I want to remember the great love and joy that this mother has for her daughters. I would want someone to throw a party for me if I had been lost and was found. I would want someone to love me if I were the more serious and easily offended type like the older sister. It seems like an important story for us to remember because any one of us might get lost and need to be found. Or any one of us might be more like the older sister and feel offended because the younger sister was getting so much attention. All of us need the kind of love this extravagant mother was offering her daughters, a love bigger than words can say. Will you help me remember that our God is a God of love? Our God is just like this axtravagant mother. I can see her at the kitchen window, drying dishes, waiting and watching for me and you to come home.

25

Mary Magdalene

LUKE 24:1–12

A very long time ago there lived a little girl named Mary Magdalene. She was a good girl. Her mother was proud of her. But Mary's mother worried about her daughter sometimes. Mary's right hip was not formed properly before she was born. That hip caused her right leg to be shorter than the left leg. That short leg caused Mary to walk with a limp. She took a step and then dragged her leg, stepped then dragged, stepped then dragged. Walking with Mary could be slow and tedious, and for that reason other children sometimes ran ahead of Mary, leaving her far behind where she had to learn to entertain herself. Mary often felt badly about herself. She could not go to school because she was a girl. Her mother taught her about cooking and cleaning, the things that girls were allowed to learn. But Mary was even slow about learning that sort of thing. She thought she was just plain stupid. Mary grew up with a deep wish to be something other than slow and stupid.

Mary was at home, as usual, on the day Jesus first visited her family. He was staying in Mary's town for a while, teaching, healing, and attending worship at the synagogue. Mary was so proud to have Jesus staying with her family. He was fun to have around. He sat at the table and enjoyed meals with Mary and her brothers, her father and mother. He taught Mary how to play several games and she was amazed to be the winner more than once! He told wonderful stories and invited Mary to tell stories of her own. She felt so good while Jesus was visiting! Mary noticed, as she said, "Good-bye!" and watched Jesus traveling on to the next town, that she felt more special than she had ever felt before. "I did not feel slow or dumb one time while Jesus was here!" she exclaimed to her mother.

Several years went by and Mary grew older. Jesus visited several times in her home over the years. But Mary could never have imagined what would finally happen to Jesus. She was there with all of the other women, standing still and frozen with grief at the foot of the cross while Jesus slowly died in terrible pain. It was too awful. Mary wanted to die with Jesus rather than to go on living in a world without him, in a world where someone so kind and good could be treated so badly.

The men who had been closest to Jesus were hiding behind locked doors somewhere in town. They were afraid that they would be crucified as Jesus was crucified. Mary and the other girls and women were hardly noticed by the guards and the people of authority. Women and children were not important people to the guards and authorities on that day. So women and children were there to see with their own eyes what happened to Jesus. Mary watched as a man named Joseph from a place called Arimathea took the dead body of Jesus, lovingly wrapped it in a linen cloth, and carried the body to a cemetery and a grave. This grave was made from a hole dug into a rocky hillside. It was not a grave like we think of graves, a hole dug straight down into the dirt. But the grave for the body of Jesus was more like a cave, a grave in which Joseph could stand up straight as he carried the lifeless body to rest on a shelf made of rock. The police rolled a huge stone over the opening into the grave.

Mary did not know what to do with her sadness. It kept rolling over her and knocking her down. She wanted Jesus to come back, to sit at the table with her and her family, to play games, and to laugh. But since Jesus was dead, Mary knew it could not happen. The best she could hope for now was to be close to the body of Jesus. She waited until after the Sabbath Day had passed. Then she took a bottle of anointing oil and fresh herbs to the grave where she had seen Joseph leaving the body of Jesus. Oils and herbs were gifts given to loved ones who had died, precious gifts used to express love and adoration. Mary wanted to put the oils and herbs on the body of Jesus, something special, gifts she could share to try and say how much Jesus meant to her.

The early morning light filtered softly through the tree branches and shrubs around the grave. Morning birds cooed and rabbits hopped out of Mary's way as she stepped then dragged, stepped then dragged, stepped then dragged to the cemetery. She hoped to find guards willing to remove the stone that sealed the opening to Jesus' grave. But she was surprised to see that the stone was already rolled back from the grave when she arrived. Mary leaned over to look inside the grave. The grave was empty. There was no body inside. Mary saw the linen cloth that Joseph had used to wrap Jesus' body. It was neatly folded. Mary jumped back with fear. She wondered what had happened and then she saw two men, huge and dazzling like angels. "Why are you looking in a grave for someone who is very much alive?" one of the smiling angels asked Mary. "You are looking for Jesus and he was dead. He was in this grave for three days. But he is no longer here. He is no longer dead. He is alive."

Mary shivered all over. What an amazing morning! Suddenly the sun was brighter and the birds cooed more happily. Rabbits, squirrels, and raccoons came to look closely at the angels in their dazzling robes. "I've got to go tell the disciples!" Mary shrieked. Step, drag, step, drag, step, drag, step drag! As fast as her legs would carry her, Mary rushed to the locked room where the disciples were hiding. Mary knocked loudly. She heard many dead bolts being unlocked and many barricades being lifted. The door opened and Mary jumped inside the room to announce joyfully, "Jesus is no longer dead! He is out of the grave and alive!"

The disciples looked sternly at Mary Magdalene through the dim lantern light in their hiding place. She could see that they thought she was crazy. Peter got up from his seat and looked more closely into Mary's face. He began to remember some of the things that Jesus had said. Jesus had said strange things about dying and coming back to life. Peter began to run! He ran all the way to the grave and looked inside. Mary had been telling the truth. Jesus was no longer in the grave. Only the linen cloth was left where the body had been.

Mary Magdalene was the first Easter person, the first one to be told the good news that has brought us all together as church people. Here we are and more than two thousand years have gone by. We are still celebrating the good news that Mary Magdalene brought to the disciples of Jesus. He is alive. He is not dead. We are the church, the people who still tell about the empty grave. It is a story first told by a girl who long ago wished that she were something other than slow and stupid.

Will you help me to remember what a difference Mary's friendship with Jesus made in her life? I hope that we are the kind of people who will stay close to Jesus. I hope we are the kind of church that will continue to announce the good news that Jesus is still alive. His friendship and love can make all of us feel how special we are... forever.

26

Wind and Fire

ACTS 2

It happened about two thousand years ago and that's a very long time. A boy by the name of Derek stood at his mother's side and watched when Jesus was crucified. He was holding his mother's hand when they looked into the tomb and saw that the body of Jesus was no longer inside. The boy heard with his own ears when the angel spoke to the entire group of women and children, saying that Jesus was no longer with the dead but among the living. Derek was amazed at all that was going on. His mother could not answer his questions fast enough. "What does it mean to be among the dead?" he asked. "What does it mean to rise from the dead?" He pulled on his mother's arm as they ran into the town. His mother wanted to tell others what they had seen even though she could not answer all Derek's questions. It was an amazing time. Everyone was so excited.

In spite of the amazement and joy, people were scared. Derek could see the fear in adult eyes. He could hear fear behind their words. And there was joy too. The people were gathering in homes and on the lakeshores. They were singing new songs with voices that sounded refreshed and strong. Derek was learning as all of us learn while growing up. People said that nothing like this had ever happened before. Everything was so unexpected. The friends of Jesus had been shocked to see him killed. They were not expecting him to come to life again. And later, when he stood among them, eating fish and talking about a Holy Spirit, they had no idea what might happen next. Derek stood beside his mother when Jesus went up into heaven, saw Jesus' feet leave the ground and go higher and higher as if the man was attached to a cluster of helium balloons. "Wow!" was all that Derek could think to say that day. It was all so amazing. Derek kept asking over and over, "How did he do that?" Not a single adult had an answer for the boy.

Fifty days had passed since the night when Jesus was arrested and taken into custody. It was the Sabbath Day, and Derek went with his mother to worship with others who had heard Jesus preach. A large crowd was gathered that day. The disciples of Jesus were there. People who had been healed by Jesus were telling their stories. Derek heard much talking. He could not understand all that was being said because there were people gathered from many different places. The boy heard foreign languages being spoken as he walked at his mother's side. She was looking for her brothers and sisters, moving through the crowd.

Just as Derek and his mother found their family and friends, there was a rumble and a rush. Violent winds blew and all hats were blown away, tumbling into the distance before anyone could reach for them. Scarves on the women's heads stood straight out like starched flags. Then the fires appeared. Flames of fire stood over the heads of the men and women who were gathered together. The fire burned brightly, red hot, but no one was burned. People were amazed. They said to each other, "What is this?" And no matter what language a person spoke, they were all able to understand each other. There was no such thing as a foreign language. It was as if a Spanish-speaking man was there and he could understand the man next to him who was speaking French. Or as if a Russian woman was standing beside a Japanese woman and both of them could understand each other as if they were speaking the same language. Every word that was spoken while the fire burned was a word clearly understood by the entire crowd. Even Derek understood the language of the adults!

It was the most amazing worship service Derek had ever seen. All people seemed like family and friends. The fear that had creased his mother's forehead disappeared. Derek saw only joy in the adult faces that surrounded him. People from far away places spoke to Derek in his own language, asking him if he had known Jesus. It was great fun to start talking in his own Galilean language, "Yes, I know Jesus. He ate dinner with us many times." Derek heard his voice going out to others in a language that they understood. The language was not Galilean! "Wow!" What else could the boy say? "Wow!" He said it again because he simply had to say something. And everyone understood "Wow!" just as it was spoken in every language represented there. Everyone was amazed.

The wind and the fire brought more than amazement that day. The Holy Spirit came with the wind and flames. God's Spirit came to live in those who knew and worshiped Jesus. The Holy Spirit of God, the same Spirit that had been in Jesus, came to live in Jesus' followers. That Spirit gave them courage. The day was called Pentecost and from that very day, the day that made Derek say "Wow!" to this very day, the people of Jesus have passed on the courage of God's Holy Spirit.

Derek walked home with his mother, his family, and his friends from that Sabbath Day worship experience and he saw no more fear in his mother's face, no more fear in his grandfather's face, no more fear in his neighbor's face. Derek felt great courage rising in his own body. It made his shoulders straight and set his chin up high. He was looking up into the sky as he walked home, wondering what in the world the Holy Spirit would do among the people he knew and loved.

Pentecost Sunday marks the beginning of the church as we know it. It took great power and courage for people to build the church of Jesus Christ. It takes great power and courage for us, still, to worship and live as witnesses to the love and goodness of Jesus. Will you help me to remember that we have the Holy Spirit within us? We have the same power that Derek had, the power that amazed him and took fear from the faces of his family and friends. Don't be afraid. The power of God is in you. The power of God is in all of us.

Other books from The Pilgrim Press

Adult worship services can be uplifting and inspiring for adults, but difficult for children. Our collection of children's sermons insures that worship can be uplifting and inspiring for the young among us. Choose from our selection of children's sermons that include the lectionary-based *Time with Our Children*, the smorgasbord of age-appropriate messages presented by *The Brown Bag*, or the celebration of children in *Small Wonders*.

WIPE THE TEARS
30 Children's Sermons on Death
Phyllis Vos Wezeman, Anna L. Liechty, and Kenneth R. Wezeman
ISBN 0-8298-1520-1 • 96 pages • paper • $10.00

TOUCH THE WATER
30 Children's Sermons on Baptism
Phyllis Vos Wezeman, Anna L. Liechty, and Kenneth R. Wezeman
ISBN 0-8298-1518-X • 96 pages • paper • $10.00

TASTE THE BREAD
30 Children's Sermons on Communion
Phyllis Vos Wezeman, Anna L. Liechty, and Kenneth R. Wezeman
ISBN 0-8298-1519-8 • 96 pages • paper • $10.00

PLANTINGS SEEDS OF FAITH
Virginia H. Loewen
ISBN 0-8298-1473-6 • 96 pages • paper • $10.00

GROWING SEEDS OF FAITH
Virginia H. Loewen
ISBN 0-8298-1488-4 • 96 pages • paper • $10.00

THE BROWN BAG
Jerry Marshall Jordan
ISBN 0-8298-0411-0 • 117 pages • paper • $9.95

SMALL WONDERS
Sermons for Children
Glen E. Rainsley
ISBN 0-8298-1252-0 • 104 pages • paper • $13.00

TIME WITH OUR CHILDREN
Stories for Use in Worship, Year A
Dianne E. Deming
ISBN 0-8298-0941-4 • 160 pages • paper • $13.00

TIME WITH OUR CHILDREN
Stories for Use in Worship, Year B
Dianne E. Deming
ISBN 0-8298-0952-X • 182 pages • paper • $13.00

TIME WITH OUR CHILDREN
Stories for Use in Worship, Year C
Dianne E. Deming
ISBN 0-8298-0953-8 • 157 pages • paper • $13.00

To order these or any other books from The Pilgrim Press call or write to:

THE PILGRIM PRESS
700 Prospect Avenue East
Cleveland, Ohio 44115-1100

Phone orders: 1-800-537-3394 • Fax orders: 216-736-2206
Please include shipping charges of $4.00 for the first book and
75¢ for each additional book.
Or order from our web sites at www.thepilgrimpress.com and www.ucpress.com.

Prices subject to change without notice.